D0368477

SOLVING PUBLIC RELATIONS PROBLEMS

by **VERNE BURNETT**

SOLVING
PUBLIC RELATIONS
PROBLEMS

B. C. FORBES & SONS PUBLISHING CO., INC.
80 FIFTH AVENUE, NEW YORK, N.Y.

HD59
.B8

Copyright, 1952, by B. C. Forbes & Sons Publishing Company, Inc.

ALL RIGHTS RESERVED

No part of this book may be reproduced in any form without permission in writing from the publisher.

Printed in the United States of America
Country Life Press Corp., Garden City, New York

Preface

WHILE VISITING WITH A FRIEND who does public relations work, I mentioned that I had made some notes of potential value, in book form, to other people interested in this field.

In discussing my material, we observed that a good deal of it applies to analyzing problems and to planning strategy and programs for solving such problems. It does not emphasize the details of operating a program, but the thinking and planning required before throwing on a switch to put the program into motion.

As we continued our talk, an idea began to emerge—the availability of a more or less basic formula for understanding and solving a problem in public relations. Examples illustrate each step in the formula—how to apply it and why.

Some of the illustrations actually happened as described. Many had to be telescoped in order to concentrate upon certain points. Some examples have been deliberately changed to emphasize a point and to get to it directly. In a few cases the author made projections to show what he thinks should be done.

Names are entirely fictitious, except where clearly identified. Titles of corporations and companies follow the alphabet, from A to S. Fictitious names of persons employ colors such as Black, Brown, Gray, Green, and White; directions such as North, West, Southern, and Easterly; random names from the telephone book chosen alphabetically, running from Abbott through Thomson. A few others like Jones and Smith, Bill and Mary, do not represent any special person but provide a little more readability.

Many illustrations apply to complicated situations in the midst

AUG 21 1984

of pressure and tension. With conflicting viewpoints, Mr. A may recall the anecdotes quite differently from Mr. B. But all the examples either reflect what actually took place or represent what can and does happen or should happen.

There is nothing but good will and understanding intended in regard to the actors in these briefly told incidents. In fact, I want to extend my heartfelt appreciation to all these men and women. Without exception, they helped in developing a better understanding of public relations and in showing how better to approach and solve a public relations problem.

Many persons have contributed to the ideas expressed in this book, including clients, business associates, employes, editors and writers, and numberless other persons. Thanks to all of them! Also, I hope that they will like to have some of their experiences and knowledge passed along to others who may benefit.

I want to thank especially several publications for giving me permission to quote excerpts of their material.

Verne Burnett

Foreword

I T HAS BEEN my good fortune for many years to meet leaders in Industry, Business, Finance, and discuss with them the whys and wherefores of human relations.

Those who direct our corporations for the benefit of share-owners, consumers, labor, management, have social responsibilities and obligations beyond making a fair return on invested capital.

I quote the following, as pertinent today as at the time of utterance, in 1919, by B. C. Forbes:

> Unless business can win the approval of the people, it will find itself checkmated and thwarted sooner or later. As much regard must hereafter be paid to the people as to profits. The earners of profits must have a new regard for public sentiment, for the public's feeling, the public's attitude, the public's wellbeing.

We have come a long way since then. Enlightened present-day leaders recognize the value of better human relations. Men have been trained in the science of public—human—relations and are helping these leaders to put forth conscientious efforts for the over-all good of the community.

It is widely recognized today that there is spiritual as well as financial value in applying these principles as a continuing policy.

Verne Burnett, author of this book, thoroughly discusses the spiritual side, with practical demonstrations of public relations fundamentals.

I remember meeting Verne for the first time, when, as Vice President of General Foods he was "Director of Public Relations", then a relatively new title in industry. He was making good use of his studious, researching ability for the corporate good; I was spreading the Gospel of the Good Life in Business. He was most helpful to me.

This book has much to offer to newcomers to the field of public relations, who will gain a great deal of knowledge, as well as to leaders who can be guided further by the experiences of the author whose life's work is back of this volume and who, himself, has not stopped learning.

May I add that the subject is not new. I quote:

> So likewise ye, except ye utter by the tongue words easy to be understood, how shall it be known what is spoken? for ye shall speak into the air.

More power to you, Verne Burnett, in your helping of others!

FRANK H. BURNS

Introduction

M R. JONES PIONEERED in the field of public relations. Starting shortly after World War I, he studied existing techniques, and, like other pioneers, created and tested many new ideas and methods.

At the same time that public relations work grew more widespread and complex, Mr. Jones found certain phases of it becoming more clear-cut. In a sense, he felt like a farmer searching in a thicket for a spring of drinking water. He aimed to cut through a great deal of non-essential underbrush—quickly and expertly —to arrive at his goal.

The spring in public relations consists of the heart of a problem and its solution. These are the most important to find and, for the untrained, they are the most difficult. When the spring is found, its presence and nature often seem amazingly obvious. The brier patch surrounding it had appeared too thick and out of proportion from the close-up, ground-eye view. Public relations, with its trained objectivity, provides a kind of mental helicopter. In addition, it has the tools and skills for doing the clean-up job.

Mr. Jones discovered a basic formula for seeking out the nub of a complex problem and learning how to solve it. This formula needs adjusting, of course, to fit different circumstances. But time after time it has met with success.

To explain the formula is the aim of this book, in the hope that it will be of interest to every thoughtful person, but particularly to the following:

1. Someone who wants to know how to acquire basic public relations knowledge as part of his education.

2. A person considering a career for himself in public relations.

3. An individual already doing work in public relations or an allied field, such as advertising or journalism, who would like to know more about how to apply the principles and techniques of public relations.

4. An executive or group leader who wants to understand better how to analyze human relations problems and how to go about trying to solve them.

Public Relations is as far flung as humanity itself. Naturally, the author could have firsthand knowledge of only limited segments. They include chiefly those of business and its ramifications, which spread out like the spokes of a Ferris wheel. They apply to employes and their home towns; stockholders; suppliers; distributors and dealers, and many services such as utilities and transport needed in the making of products and getting them to consumers.

Business contributes to countless churches, schools, hospitals, charities, and other agencies dealing with public welfare and public information; thousands of trade associations, professional societies, and service and other organizations in which business plays an important role. To spend money intelligently for memberships or donations, business must learn something about the work of the recipients.

Dealings with government occur on every level from a New England town meeting up to Capitol Hill, and branching out to all countries this side of the Iron Curtain.

The most vital human relationships for many businesses concern vast numbers of customers or large special groups. Therefore, business should learn how to work with opinion research, opinion molders, and media such as publications, broadcasting, direct mail, motion pictures, posters, and word-of-mouth.

The hub of this giant wheel of human relationships is correct analysis and wise handling of various problems. On this hub our book will largely concentrate.

First, the reader should make sure that he has a fair understanding of the fundamental nature and purpose of public relations. If a person cannot get for himself a sufficient grasp of public relations, he should call for the aid of some well-qualified person. The more one knows about this subject, the more useful he becomes. Our first chapter will deal with an understanding of public relations.

•   •   •

Two Definitions of Public Relations

I N WEBSTER'S NEW INTERNATIONAL DICTIONARY, 1949, the following definitions are given of public relations:

1. "The activities of an industry, union, corporation, profession, government, or other organization, in building and maintaining sound and productive relations with special publics, such as customers, employes or stockholders, and with the public at large, so as to adapt itself to its environment and interpret itself to society."

2. "The state of such activities, or the degree of their success, in furthering public understanding of an organization's economic and social adjustment; as, good or poor *public relations.*"

3. "The art or profession of organizing and developing these activities; as, university courses in *public relations;* public relations requires technical skill in various techniques. Hence, *public relations officer, director, counsel, or consultant.*"

• • •

The editors of *Public Relations News* have defined public relations in this manner:

"Public Relations is the management function which evaluates public attitudes, identifies the policies and procedures of an individual or an organization with the public interest, and executes a program of action to earn public understanding and acceptance."

Contents

CHAPTER I } A Broad Understanding of Public Relations

M ODERN PUBLIC RELATIONS started shortly before the home radio set. Essential phases of public relations, of course, appeared throughout history. As a well-defined field of activity it arrived in the Twentieth Century. Most of the development has occurred since around 1920.

The power of public relations in its broadest meaning has proved itself in every phase of human relationships, ranging from propaganda on a world-wide basis to an individual's contacts with his family and neighborhood.

You can find dozens of helpful definitions but for our purpose the heart of them consists of "live right and be understood." What you are and do should be wedded with what you say.

• • •

Let's begin with an example of a personal nature: The daughter of wealthy and powerful parents received a great deal of publicity, much of it unfavorable. Because of her family's prominence many things she did and said in public became news. Naturally, she preferred to have favorable publicity but overlooked the simple fact that her conduct formed the starting point in her public relations. Her expensive way of living, her marital troubles, and her comments to the press caused unpleasant effects.

Later on, a wise member of the family used a keen grasp of public relations in guiding another relative—a young girl. The girl, while attending college, dressed pretty much like her classmates and did not make a display of expensive furs and jewels.

1

Her allowance of spending money stayed fairly well in line with that of the average student. She behaved in a modest and friendly, not patronizing, manner. She appeared in public only in wholesome surroundings. Should she be asked to pose for a news photographer or make a statement to the press, she knew how to act with good judgment.

Under this regime, she actually had fun and got a good education—without notoriety. After graduation, she entered the career of her choice and succeeded in her work. Her wedding occurred without undue fanfare and she could look forward to a reasonably happy and normal life.

The young woman, in spite of a high-spirited and independent nature, had the intelligence to accept sound public relations advice, the basis of which is consideration of what you are and do as well as what you say.

•   •   •

Turning from this personal example to group activities, we find that leaders of nearly all kinds of organizations recognize values in public relations. Most of these leaders know something about the subject, but they seldom have a well-rounded comprehension. Large gaps must be filled before such persons really can understand public relations and get the full benefit.

You should make sure to *deserve* good will before trying to win public understanding and approval. Yet, time after time a leader of an organization will insist on pursuing only the latter phase.

The management of one corporation became noted for making mistakes on national and international levels. After indulging in such mistakes, it would spend a great deal of money for advertising and editorial publicity projects to mollify the wrath of officialdom and the disgust of the public. Finally, the corporation took into its top management a person trained in *anticipating* public reactions. The management paid attention to this specialist and thereby headed off most of its troubles with public opinion.

•   •   •

Shortly before Hitler invaded Poland, an American corporation considered doing business with the Nazis. The proponents in the corporate management stated that it could earn millions of dollars of profit. They said other American companies had done business in Germany for many years, and no resentment resulted in the United States therefrom. Also, an affiliate in a non-Nazi country would handle the business arrangement.

The corporation's public relations officer took the position that, after Hitler had come into power in Germany, nearly everyone in the United States was opposed to him and what he stood for. Any profit possibility in Europe would be more than offset by loss of business from American distributors, dealers, and the public because of their resentment at dealing with Hitler. The customers and stockholders of the corporation would regard the arrangement as unethical, unwise, and in bad taste.

Many American companies which had invested in activities in Germany before Hitler's rise had done so with the blessing of Washington, D. C., and were exempt from public disapproval. Working through a non-Nazi affiliate abroad would not affect the principle. World War II, then imminent, would void the business arrangement with the Nazis.

If the war in Europe had not broken out and the business deal had been made, the public relations personnel would have been expected to smooth over angry public reactions—with considerable expense and effort and with no assurance of success. One of the greatest services of public relations is to anticipate potential trouble and make sure it doesn't strike.

•   •   •

To prevent ill will and to build good will, a person or organization should not rely on a smattering of public relations knowledge. If you plan to have a serious operation performed, you will not call in a medical student who has yet to win his degree and serve his internship. And you will probably not accept medical advice from an untrained person merely because he feels he has valuable intuitions regarding diagnosis and treatment.

Dealing with the human mind and emotions, opinions, and attitudes, especially with large, ramified groups, involves fully as much difficulty as analyzing and prescribing for a physical ailment.

Mr. Smith, a clothing manufacturer, recognized vaguely the values of good human relations. He read magazine articles, heard speeches at trade group meetings, and discussed the subject at his luncheon club.

With a desire to be of service to his community in which hundreds of his employes lived, he accepted the chairmanship of the board of directors of a principal local charity. Due to no fault of his own, the charitable organization had become involved in a controversy.

In an address to a large group of contributors to the charity, he said: "I believe in good public relations. First, I find out what people really think and feel. So, I have talked with several of my employes about the issue before us today. I briefed them on my position. They agreed with me unanimously. . . ."

Of course they did! Probably some of them really sympathized with his viewpoint. Others could see no benefit in offending a boss with a mind obviously closed. He lacked objectivity and did not use even the rudiments of public opinion research. He realized there was powerful force in public opinion but did not call for skilled aid in exploring it.

The decisive vote of the contributors against Mr. Smith's

stand caused him to look more deeply into public opinion research and to use experienced assistance to carry out his desire to comprehend public opinion.

. . .

Mr. Black, a cosmetics manufacturer, also realized that public relations exercised great power in modern business and society. He gained a spotty impression of the nature of this power and how to use it. He had attended public relations conferences where he listened to the speeches with keen interest. Also, he did some good reading. Without trained guidance, however, he initiated a sizable public relations program.

He gave inadequate thought to his company's real public relations problems, to the correction of internal abuses, to the theme he wished to have accepted by the public, and to the methods. He energetically by-passed such essential preliminaries and concentrated on trying to get quickly the end result of public good will. Instead, he offended editors and made other mistakes.

Following this fiasco, he employed competent persons to form a public relations department and engaged an outstanding counseling firm. These trained persons, after a sound analysis of the problem, built a program and set it in motion. In due time, the good will he sought began to emerge.

. . .

The chairman of a hardware products corporation knew about phases of public relations but thought the counsel should stay entirely under his direction, enmeshed in the internal details of the organization, and hence without objectivity. A public relations counsel needs to understand essential facts about an organization, its policies, practices, and key personnel. But, also, he must know how people outside of the management think, and how to correlate the two.

In Review

To summarize this chapter, acquire a broad understanding of public relations before attempting to analyze and solve a problem. Or, someone who does have such understanding should supply guidance. The keystone of public relations is the character and conduct of a person or organization. The remainder of the arch is largely interpretation. This applies equally to an individual such as the young woman of social prominence or to the management of a great organization.

Some executives use only the interpretative phases of public relations in an effort to gloss over mistakes, or to erect a pleasing facade with insufficient regard for what lies behind it.

Give thought to the *anticipation* of reactions of the general public or special publics.

In working with human relations, relying on insufficient knowledge proves as hazardous as dealing with a charlatan in case of a disease.

In addition to the value of thorough training, a public relations practitioner contributes objectivity and impartiality in his approach to any problem.

With these basic approaches to the meaning of public relations, we now proceed to explore a few of the most fundamental factors of human nature with which we must work.

CHAPTER II } Fundamental Factors of Human Nature

A CUPFUL OF GASOLINE contains a vast array of atoms. An expert can tell you what will happen to the mixture as a whole when the gas gets into the engine of your car and ignites. But one individual atom may not behave exactly like the others. Exceptions to usual behavior occur in plant and animal life. And with human beings the variations from customary group conduct seem much more numerous.

In public relations work, one must learn a great deal about both the mass and the single atom. A multitude of human beings will usually act in a fairly predictable manner. To a considerable extent, though less so, this is true of a person. Since we deal both with groups and with individuals, we must have some knowledge of each. To get such knowledge requires study and experience.

A public relations practitioner needs to have an insight into various human relations subjects, examples of which we will discuss in this chapter. Also a top-level executive should have at least an awareness of them and some grasp of their fundamentals.

Knowing Oneself

To understand other people *know yourself*. In public relations work many times you, like other persons, will have to put your intellect and objective judgment into one room and lock your emotions in a padded cell.

A public relations problem, in a sense, forms a series of circles, some concentric and some overlapping. At the center is your client, or really yourself, acting in his behalf. So, there are numerous factors you should know about yourself in order to deal properly with human relations.

As a boy, James noticed that his father had a trait which seemed unusual. The father changed jobs several times and each time, he would quickly decide that certain employes were going to be hostile to him. He would come home and describe his suspicions about the persons he had elected as potential opponents. As you might well guess, his own attitude toward those individuals caused them to dislike him.

As James grew up, he discovered himself following his father's pattern. He realized that he needlessly created hostility instead of good will. In starting one job, he found himself taking such an intense dislike to a new associate, a Mr. Ring, that he said to himself, "This is wrong and it must be changed." He decided he would try to understand his own reactions and those of his new associates.

He realized that he had fallen into his father's unfortunate habit. So, he decided to listen sympathetically to Mr. Ring and learn why he seemed to be offensive. He found that Mr. Ring had had a long series of failures and rebuffs. To offset these he had become boastful and highly aggressive. After James understood the background, Mr. Ring's boasts and aggressive actions seemed more pathetic than irritating.

An enduring friendship grew up between Mr. Ring and James. Mr. Ring sensed that James understood and appreciated him. Also James realized he had discovered a big step in human relations—understanding himself and his reactions to persons around him.

•   •   •

A paper products corporation, always expanding, needed new capital from investors. The public relations counselor studied the attitudes of the stockholders and found that many of them resented the large bonuses given to the officers. He told this to the president of the company and received an angry look. But the president could quickly put aside his personal feelings, as he had an excellent understanding of himself.

He agreed that bonuses to himself and his fellow officers should be in line with accepted practice. He authorized a study by an independent expert and reported the results to his stockholders. Actually, the bonuses were not out of line and stockholder complaints practically ceased.

* * *

An understanding of yourself helps in countless ways. You must know why you get angry or boast or interrupt people. Thus you learn how to get along better within yourself and with others. You get an idea of what goes on inside *them*.

One executive had an overpowering urge to attract favorable attention for himself, so he made many speeches—too many. He didn't realize that he used his energies in a drive for personal glory, instead of devoting them to gaining credit for his company and its products. His vanity kept his judgment out of focus.

A public relations practitioner should not be too introspective. But he should know something about the nature of his emotions and their effects on his judgment. This does not mean that a public relations worker should try to pose as an authority on psychiatry. But he should give some thought to self-understanding, in order to develop his objectivity.

The Drive for Attention

Long ago Dr. Sigmund Freud and others began to examine the driving force, for good and bad, of the inferiority complex in the individual. A knowledge of this force, both with the human being as well as with large groups of persons, including nations, forms a vital part of background knowledge needed for public relations work.

The terrific changes affecting the lives of people in recent generations have had numerous impacts on the minds, emotions, and complexes of human beings, singly and in groups.

In the 1930's a mentally alert New Englander of 85 years told about his boyhood days when his grandfather walked with him around his neighborhood and related the history of each home and family. The grandfather had been alive before General Cornwallis surrendered at Yorktown in 1781. One single leap from the recent past to the American Revolution! But what changes in our ways of living and working since then! These changes, especially in the last two or three generations, and even during the past decade, have rushed in too rapidly for some people to adjust themselves.

·   ·   ·

We should study the inferiority and other complexes, both for one person and a large aggregation, against the background of radical alterations in our lives due to modern science, business, education, and politics. A public relations worker seldom has the benefit of training in psychology or psychoanalysis, but he should acquire certain knowledge in those fields.

One effect of our swiftly changing world has been widespread frustrations in the individual in his quest for glory, power, and wealth. Neuroses always have existed but until recent times few seemed to be aware of their nature and how to cope with them. Today, many who deal with public opinion have an awareness of frustrations and neuroses on both a personal and a mass basis.

·   ·   ·

Mr. Brown works in a factory. Earlier, in high school, he called the signals for his football team and felt like an important person. He went through a state of adolescent revolt against the authority of his parents and teachers. He didn't expect to be President of the United States but did have ideas about how to handle the job. At least he expected to attain a fair amount of riches, power, and fame, and popularity with both men and women when he grew up and went to work.

During his working hours at the factory, however, he discovered he didn't call any of the signals. His foreman did. Over the foreman there arose in ascending rank a general foreman, a works manager, a divisional vice president, and on up through the hierarchy to the chairman of the board and the stockholders. Also, a shop steward, and other local, regional and national officials of the labor union.

Instead of acting as a member of a small group, such as the clerks in a grocery store where he once had worked during a summer vacation, and where he felt he got a reasonable share of attention, Mr. Brown now sensed the enormous weight and power of a great corporation which made him feel small and cramped in contrast. Some of his fellow-workers didn't react to the situation the same as Mr. Brown, but others did.

He regarded big business as a good thing for the country— for its security and its economy. He sometimes liked to boast to friends about his Company, spelled with a capital C. But emotionally he couldn't quite adjust himself as an individual to the modern scheme of things with so much bigness and so much remoteness from the boss. As a grocery clerk relations were close and simple—he had called his employer "Joe."

Mr. Brown worked on an assembly line. He had responsibility only for one tiny item in a long chain of operations needed for the finished product. His grandfather had worked in a small factory which made lawn mowers. The grandfather handled only a few parts of the lawn mowers but he understood the complete product. He felt the joy of craftsmanship and a sense of the wholeness of the mower and the service it rendered. In his small group the feeling of team play prevailed. With several skills instead of just one he did not get bored by monotony. To a large extent the man mastered the machine—not the reverse.

Mr. Brown realized that his grandfather had fewer advantages than himself, in many ways. The older man's hours had been longer and physically more strenuous; his purchasing power lower and employe benefits scarcer.

A period of sweeping industrial, political, and social revolution had swept in and it was difficult for young Mr. Brown to adapt himself. He felt unimportant, not noticed, and not getting ahead in the world as much as he expected. The resulting frustration and disillusionment created a degree of irritation and resentment. This showed up in his comments at meetings of his labor union, in his attitudes toward community and national affairs, and in his conversation at home and with neighbors.

While Mr. Brown does not typify a majority of Americans, he does represent a segment so large that it must be reckoned with in many human relations problems.

•   •   •

Incidentally, what can business management do to help Mr. Brown? There are countless ways.

For example, Company A, which makes cleansing products for home use, has 1000 factory and office employes. (Larger companies can apply Company A's ideas in many cases by decentralizing its managerial functions pertaining to human relations.) The chairman of the board and the president hold a series of luncheons with all employes, in groups of 30 to 40. The executives, after years of training, know the names and something about nearly every employe as an individual human being. Everyone is called, and in fact is treated as, "an associate," in a team effort.

At the so-called "understanding luncheons" the executives explain with visual aids the state of the company's business, its problems, competition, failures, and successes. They tell how much money comes in and how it goes out. They encourage questions and answer them well.

Through a variety of methods the associates become both well-informed and enthusiastic. When a group of personnel administration students called at the plant, they addressed their questions to rank-and-file workers who knew the correct answers to all questions asked about industrial relations in the plant.

Each associate in the factory learns two or more skills. When he regards one job as too monotonous, his foreman arranges to switch him to another operation for a while. Groups on assembly lines set the speed at which they can most comfortably and profitably do their jobs. The workers often set a faster speed than the management would consider suggesting.

In case of layoffs, in this company the workers, through their organization, suggest which individuals and families would suffer the least from dropping off the payroll for a short time. The welfare of the company, of course, gets full consideration. Both a husband and wife, without dependent children, may be on payrolls, and if one of these two workers were to be laid off there would be less hardship than in the case of a single breadwinner in a family with several young children. The management has veto power regarding the recommendations, but invariably finds the employes' suggestions about layoffs both humane and wise.

In many enterprises this idea might be impractical, but in Company A it works.

Company A has a profit-sharing plan which pays because it is thoroughly understood and appreciated, productive both for the workers and the stockholders. Accidents and absenteeism are almost nil. So are carelessness and waste of effort and materials. But the principal ingredient in this formula for good human relations is recognition of the individual human being with his natural desire for attention and appreciation of his problems. He wants to "be in the know" and a "member of the team."

The techniques of Company A naturally would need altering before application elsewhere, to suit individual needs. The basic point is that successful adjustments of the individual to radically changed conditions of modern times are possible and practicable, as well as necessary.

The Urge for Security

Human beings always have wanted security. The desire today is keen and has taken on new and changed forms. An understanding of this force is an important factor in solving certain public relations problems.

Millions are of the opinion that their lives, homes, and places of employment may be snuffed out at any moment in a huge atomic flash. Looking back upon the colossal efforts and sacrifices of World War II, which should have ended tyranny, they know that dictatorship has spread. Nearly everyone realizes the dangers of Communism, Socialism, Statism, and the conflicts they create. Social security provided by government looks small against the background of high prices. Many personal annuity policies and retirement funds set up by businesses seem inadequate in the face of inflation.

Most employes do not understand the legalistic language in retirement plan booklets. Bewilderment adds to insecurity. Managements can perform a great service by clearly interpreting the terms of such plans.

Also, they can lessen employes' feelings of insecurity by making it clear by deed and word that there will be no whimsical use of economic power in firing of workers.

Most of the public senses demoralization in political morals and efficiency. More people have joined churches than ever before. But in some respects religion, in its effects on national and international affairs, seems weakened. Religion in personal and family life can supply a powerful, constructive force, but many do not seem to realize this fact.

· · ·

Mr. and Mrs. Gray in 1940 had paid for their home and saved what seemed to them a fairly large amount of money. In the 11 years that followed, the purchasing power of the dollar dropped about one-half. The economic security they had looked forward to for their old age faded. Their home had nearly doubled in market value, but if they sold it and bought another they would not gain financially.

Mr. Gray, a middle-aged office-worker, tried to get a job elsewhere at a higher salary but found few companies interested in hiring someone of his age. Many companies had retirement programs and to hire him would prove costly.

The Grays had other insecurities such as possible illness, with loss of earning power; threat of a world war, and danger for their sons.

The only security the Grays could find existed within themselves—their religion and philosophy.

Recognition of this security could do much to relieve tensions in personal and public relations.

A wealthy industrialist has devoted a large part of his time for many years to encouraging people to gain the security which religion provides. He has enlisted the aid of many other leading businessmen.

On one occasion the chief industry in a large area faced the threat of a disastrous strike. Security became a principal appeal used in heading off the calamity. The public was shown, through advertising, publicity, and speeches, how nearly every family would suffer keenly from loss of jobs and pay. The welfare of cities, towns and the state was threatened, as well as the security of independent citizens. In this instance, the labor union was Communist-dominated and used dictatorial methods.

The clergy made a great deal of effort to preach spiritual security in the midst of the turmoil. This undoubtedly helped many people to attain more peace of mind and, hence, to think and act more calmly and wisely.

Social Trends

"Recent Social Trends," a colossal work prepared by dozens of experts, pioneered in explaining what happened in every important phase of American life in recent generations up to the early 1930's. This and later works provide a helpful background for understanding individual and group life and significant trends.

In this chapter we can only high spot a few of the most useful fields for background study. Let us select, for example, the shift from rural to urban and suburban living. In the United States the population has shifted drastically—notably toward cities and suburbs and to the West. In periods of high industrial activity, hundreds of thousands of people migrate from rural areas to the large cities. Their new ways of living and working have caused changes in their attitudes. An apartment-house dweller of today has a sharply different outlook from that of his ancestor who owned a house, paid direct taxes on his real estate, worked in his garden or on his farm, and knew his neighbors.

Most of his ancestors worked harder physically. They had fewer tensions and less complex worries. Most of them had to be personally resourceful and self-reliant on their farms or in their villages. Yet much teamwork flourished on a small, intimate scale. When a business depression occurred, people took care of each other instead of relying upon large charities or city, state, or federal governments.

·   ·   ·

Mr. and Mrs. Green grew up in a small town. As teen-agers they knew everyone for blocks around. Their mothers borrowed eggs and sugar from neighbors. Life was slow in tempo, but pleasant and natural. Then Mr. and Mrs. Green moved to a metropolis and rented an apartment.

After five years the Greens got acquainted with only two other families in the large building in which they lived. They did not take a deep interest in civic affairs and relied upon a remote and unfamiliar political machine to run their city government. Instead of owning their home and taking pride in it, they depended upon a landlord to pay the taxes and handle the upkeep of their living quarters.

This different mode of living altered the Greens' attitudes in regard to politics, charities, and social contacts. It changed their ideas about recreation, the size of their family, and the education of their children.

·   ·   ·

Each community is different. For instance, a city which has expanded slowly becomes conditioned to its way of life. An evolutionary process is at work. A city of mushroom growth is likely to have more turmoil, although it often is more receptive to new ideas.

A food company recognized this fact when it decided to make a test regarding a revolutionary, new kind of product. The company wanted to get the reactions of an urban group which would be the most representative. It didn't want the experiment in a "mining camp" city filled with recently arrived persons not at all accustomed to their new surroundings and way of life. And it didn't want a population too long established and conservative in its viewpoints. So it selected a city that happily combined various factors. The findings indicated that the company could safely embark upon distribution in many other cities.

In some public relations problems, knowledge of the nature of the rural to urban swing of population will prove valuable. This is one of the several major trends of which a public relations worker should become aware.

Economic and Social Classes

In the United States children learn that all men are created equal, that anyone can get to the top. But everyone can't be a leader. There are many inequalities among people and relatively few have what is needed to be highly successful. These truths should be recognized, especially by public relations workers, even though the admission is emotionally hard to accept.

In public relations work you need to learn certain facts about economic and social classes. First, let's examine the subject chiefly from economic and educational standpoints.

Each old American city has a small group of wealthy families whose ancestors lived in the community for generations.

A second small group, of more recent vintage, has about equal wealth and influence. In these first two classes nearly all the sons and daughters prepare in high schools or private schools for a college education.

A third class consists of above-average income and educational levels. Other groupings descend the ladder economically and in other ways until we get to those on relief rolls or, for some reason or other, with low incomes and little schooling.

Many borderline cases and exceptions come to mind but, by and large, these strata appear rather clearly, even in fairly new cities with somewhat fewer classes.

In each level we find differences in education, in what the people read, what they listen to over the radio and watch on television. Their attitudes vary in national and local politics and in many other ways. They tend to group themselves in certain churches, fraternal orders, and cultural and recreational organizations.

In dealing with public relations, especially on a community basis, you should know about these levels and their special interests if you wish to talk their language and influence them.

Professional and occupational groups call for additional study. For instance, the physician has a background different from most of his neighbors. He learned to concentrate largely on the individual patient and make allowances for anyone unable to pay the usual fees. The manufacturer must think in terms of large groups of employes, and he tries to treat all of them under a uniform set of rules. While the manufacturer and the doctor play golf and bridge together and have many other things in common, sharp clashes sometimes develop in a controversy between a medical staff of a hospital and a board of managers made up largely of local leaders in business and finance.

A public relations specialist must recognize the strata in American life, with their widely varying interests and attitudes. And he must become a character actor and immerse himself into many roles in order to understand and be understood.

Important Changes

Significant changes in America since 1929, and even since 1939, have come about so rapidly that few persons realize what has happened. For instance, two-thirds of the persons over 14 years old now are married, compared with just under 60 per cent in 1940 (54 per cent in 1900), according to the census takers.

People today get married younger than formerly. They want to have homes of their own, and this naturally has helped to make America largely a land of homeowners. The number of homeowners jumped 54 per cent between 1940 and 1950, and still climbs. More than 23 million families now own homes. Circulation of homemaking and gardening magazines increased by two-thirds in the one decade.

An idea seems to have taken hold that family life has weakened. Actually it seems stronger in various ways, especially in the case of millions of young married folks with small children. The growth of television, radio, and attractive publications has tended to keep a family together at home. Overcrowded highways and shortages of parking space have figured in many instances.

The increase in home ownership has had an effect on what goes into equipping and servicing homes. Few families today have domestic servants. So, husbands share many of the household chores. Tide Washing Clinic, sponsored by Procter & Gamble, found in a survey that 82 per cent of husbands help with washing dishes.

In one direction, family ties have loosened. Among the women working in factories, offices, and stores, more than half are married. This means that millions of wives have little time for housework. This is partly responsible for the large increase in time and labor-saving products, such as vacuum cleaners, automatic washing machines, and the use of pre-cooked foods or those which can be prepared quickly, such as frozen and canned foods.

Some of the overly zealous housework considered a "must" a generation ago is largely ignored today. Part of the necessary work is done by teen-age girls. In addition to doing housework in their own homes, a majority of them do part-time work in other homes. For instance, a study has shown that 79 per cent of the teen-age girls earn money as baby-sitters, doing errands and many other part-time jobs.

The wealth of the nation is rapidly shifting into the hands of women. They are the usual recipients of legacies and are beneficiaries of life insurance. They already own much of the stock, bonds, and real estate. Most wives nowadays live longer than their husbands. There are 1,920,000 more women than men in the United States.

One of the most sweeping changes has been in personal incomes and cost of living. Between 1940 and 1950, the average cost of living increased almost 72 per cent. But the median personal income *jumped 156 per cent*—in other words, from $789 to $2,016. In 1939, only 3.4 per cent of personal incomes exceeded $3,000 a year. Ten years later the figure rose to 26.2 per cent.

While the person with a fairly rigid income has suffered from the higher cost of living, millions of others have enjoyed an income climbing at a faster rate than their costs. Many of this latter group had previously lived more or less from hand-to-mouth and needed and wanted to buy a great many things, which they proceeded to do as their income rose.

The vast increase in the birth rate, since the early 40's, creates havoc with school facilities. About 4 million newly born infants arrived in the United States in 1950 alone. During the latter 1950's the tidal wave of youth promises to engulf colleges.

The number of graduates from high schools and colleges entering business, professions and the military has grown greatly in the past few years. This factor has a bearing on employe-employer relationships, politics, and many other fields.

The life expectancy of a human being in America has lengthened considerably. People in the age group 65–69 increased *one-third* in the 1940–1950 decade. The 70–74 age group gained one-third, while the number of persons 75 years of age or older *increased 45 per cent.* This results in a rapidly growing population of elderly people and at the same time the number of infants has reached a peak considered impossible in the 1930's.

In spite of widespread home-ownership, almost one-fifth of the people change their residence in a single year, one-third of the moves crossing county lines.

Television has spread on a spectacular scale, which has affected communication and family habits. Improvements in radio and publishing also have taken place in the same period.

With the startling increases in motorcars and other vehicles since V-J Day, many highways have become inadequate, gradually breaking up. At the same time, however, great regional networks of superhighways are taking shape. These will affect travel and national solidarity, commerce, industry, and agriculture. Expanding airline and streamlined train services draw parts of the country more closely together. In fact, improved transportation of all kinds is condensing the world into a much smaller ball.

In the field of science, amazing things take place—probably only a sample of what lies ahead. For generations the United States has led in applied research. While this activity moves ahead at an accelerated rate, fundamental or pure research also gains. Much of the progress in science seems encouraging to the public, but some strikes terror—notably in the weapons of destruction. The people realize that if American scientists can produce atomic and other fantastic weapons, persons in unfriendly countries may match them.

A widespread feeling of uncertainty and foreboding lurks, with fear of inflation and another world war. In such an atmosphere, human beings tend to huddle together like sheep. That may partially account for increased marriages and purchasing of homes. Or, young people consider marriage a good thing to be enjoyed while there is still time.

Yet there is a note of lonesomeness. The young man facing the possibility of going to war feels rather stranded—he must work out his own salvation to the limited extent he feels capable. Old people, unable to earn a livelihood and regarding themselves as a nuisance to young relatives, also feel lonely.

Among the encouraging factors, we find more knowledge about bringing up children—the hope of the world. More is understood about personal and group worries and tensions. Especially among young people, tolerance of all kinds has gained in recent years. With the sham of Communism clearly spotlighted in America, and many other countries, the internal danger from that source has greatly lessened.

Appreciation and understanding of America's particular form of capitalism and kind of government have made great strides, checking advances of socialism.

Americans have become much less insular in their thinking about world relationships. As a nation, the United States often has seemed like a "babe in the woods" in its viewpoints on international problems. But there are signs of the approach of sound maturity and acceptance of responsibility and leadership.

The public recoils at lack of integrity among public officials and wants to support corrective measures; yet petty thievery seems to have multiplied. Increase in church membership and attendance is a good sign. Another is public support at the polls recently of candidates who promised to fight corruption and wastefulness.

While public opinion seems to swing to a somewhat conservative viewpoint in politics, a kind of revolution is taking shape in some fields, notably architecture, art, and decoration.

Cycles

Many centuries ago cycles were charted in astronomy—vital in navigation of ships and development of the calendar, for example. Data piled up regarding wild life. Hudson's Bay Company found that, at regular intervals, certain animals became scarce, affecting the supply of fur. Agriculturists learned that severe winters, blights, and locusts arrived in regular patterns.

More recently, these scientific studies have turned to human beings. At regular intervals, people the world over become unusually irritable and wars reach their peaks of intensity. Public psychology, moving in waves, affects the prices of common stocks, home-building, church membership, and clothing styles. In Northern latitudes, public interest in non-fiction books reaches a peak in February and March. The top of the cycle in Southern climes occurs slightly later in the Spring. Libraries have made studies of these curves for some 20 years.

In the Spring there are more patent applications, better grades in schools, and higher marks on civil service examinations. In the Summer, intellectual interest hits its low. These facts should be known by everyone working with public relations.

The public will read and listen to some serious messages in hot weather, but usually only those of a kind which do not require maximum mental effort.

One of the most fascinating and promising elements in cycle research is in personnel relations. It is now well established that a human being has rhythms of elation or dejection. These affect industrial accidents and many other phases of employe-employer relationships.

The president of one corporation around a certain date exudes overconfidence and almost raucous cheerfulness. About six weeks later he becomes pessimistic, gloomy, and irritable. His counsel has discovered this cycle or rhythm. Accordingly, the president tries not to make important decisions at either the high or low of the swing, because he lacks his usual good judgment at those times. He also has noted fairly definite rhythms in the dispositions and general attitudes of a few of his principal lieutenants. Some of the peaks and valleys come many months apart. Some lows appear on Monday mornings and highs on Friday afternoons— week-end routines may give a clue to the answer to this one. A few persons keep their emotions so much out of view that it is almost impossible to detect the swings that are no doubt present. In any case, these rather regular fluctuations, when understood, can be beneficially utilized.

Research on cycles, spearheaded by the Foundation for the Study of Cycles, amounts only to a thimbleful thus far, as it touches human relations. But it is worth watching.

In Review

There is much to learn about human relations. We have selected a few of the more helpful studies, including the following:

1. An understanding of oneself, to gain objectivity and to get a better grasp of what other humans are like.
2. The basic urge to feel important, often thwarted and in need of adjustment to modern conditions.
3. Feeling of various kinds of insecurity, with repercussions in political, international, economic, and other fields.

4. Recent social trends, such as the switch from rural to urban living.

5. Economic, social, professional, and other groupings, with their different attitudes and interests.

6. Important recent changes occurring swiftly—rate and age of marriages; home ownership; strengthening of family life; more married women on payrolls; increase of labor saving devices; transferring of assets to women; many personal incomes growing faster than prices; increased birth rate and length of life; a much better educated public. Growth of television; more motorcars; advances of science; feeling of fear and foreboding, but also many signs giving much hope for the future.

7. Effects of cycles in human emotions and viewpoints. If for no other reason, this subject needs noting by public relations people because of the timing of the public's attention to messages which require more than usual thought.

Public relations people should draw strength from such background studies. These workers can't *specialize* in much territory beyond their own, but they at least should have insight into the essentials of several fields which deal with human relationships.

·   ·   ·

Now let us take another step along the road, to look at the priceless exhibits the field of journalism offers for public relations.

CHAPTER III } **Learn from Journalism**

A PERSON INTERESTED in public relations can draw great benefit from knowledge of journalism. If he has never worked for a newspaper or magazine, he should study several of the lessons that journalism has to offer. Top executives, too, can get good guidance from this field.

While most successful public relations practitioners have worked for a publication, other leaders did not have training in journalism, but nearly all of them have learned its fundamentals and techniques.

In 1951, General Foods Corporation conducted a mail survey on this subject among 162 public relations departments in industrial companies. Journalistic training was rated by 54 per cent (of the 74 per cent who responded) as the best preliminary training for public relations work.

To illustrate: here are some experiences of a young man called Bill who got a job as a newspaper reporter. This story does not by any means represent every newspaper and every reporter, but it states what actually happened to one person.

Bill soon remedied his initial nervousness in talking with people. After interviewing manufacturers, bankers, lawyers, merchants, politicians, labor union people, and many others, he felt at ease with anyone. A procession of lecturers, musicians, actors and other interesting persons visited the city. Bill interviewed many of them. Then there were the less pleasant assignments of questioning persons involved in crime, scandals, motor accidents, and, on rare occasions, riots, strikes, and wrecks.

His "beat" changed several times and he learned how to have some understanding of people and groups of various kinds. He had to think fast and, while not seeming to hurry, to win cooperation quickly and get to the point. Printing presses maintain a tight schedule.

Many errors, due to high speed and pressure, filter into newspapers, although accuracy is encouraged and rewarded. So, Bill formed the habit of getting the facts, trying to give a true impression of each situation and presenting the sense of it in a few words in his opening paragraph.

He sharpened his memory and learned where to get information quickly on almost any subject. Even some small newspapers have good reference sources.

Within a few years, Bill came in contact with most phases of life, including charity drives, gambling raids, court trials, religious revivals, floods, and so on and on.

A newspaper, because of its deadlines, places a premium on promptness. Bill had to learn how to get his work done on time.

At one period, he was assigned the job of writing many of the headlines. His editor asked for a two-line heading with 16 units in each line for a certain news item. This proved unusually difficult because of the long key names involved. So Bill turned back the story to the editor and said, "I am sorry, but I simply can't write this headline."

"You must," said the editor, without looking up from his work.

Bill wrote the headline.

This editor also was a stickler about style in writing. If he found a single mistake in punctuation, spelling, grammar, or use of capital letters, he would wad up the copy and throw it into a wastebasket. Red-faced, Bill would smooth the paper and puzzle out the mistake for himself, ask someone else, or check some published reference source.

While this example seems harsh, the main point is the desirability of getting work done correctly.

Bill increased his vocabulary and his skill in choosing words to convey an interesting and correct picture. Also, he learned to vary his wording to arouse and maintain interest.

Incidentally, Bill had to learn to control his temper under unpleasant circumstances. He tried to analyze what might lie back of quirks in human conduct and reactions of human beings including himself.

He learned a great deal about human relations and how to cope with them. For instance, he spent hours getting facts and writing a story about a little boy who ran away and who had a wonderful time for a day. The police had given the child ice cream cones and treated him like a crown prince. The editor considered it harmful to print the story, because other boys reading such a story, also might want to run away.

Squeamishly, Bill got facts about an unusually gruesome accident. His story was not printed because it would be offensive to many readers, and, in this particular case, serve no useful purpose.

Once Bill embellished a story with some details which might have been true, though actually only the result of his imagination. The editor sensed what had happened and instructed: "Save your make-believe for fiction."

Newspaper training taught Bill not to overplay a story. He tended to elaborate on a news item worth a paragraph by inflating it to a column. But he discovered that a simple situation occasionally has enormous human interest if he could find within it some element of novelty or emotional appeal, or opportunity for unusual treatment.

As an example of this, a former newspaper reporter started work doing publicity for a meat packer, a large producer of frankfurters, along with other products. The new publicity man could find no news worthy of sending to newspapers at that time. So he conceived a short feature item. As the Labor Day weekend arrived, he released a paragraph stating how many million hot dogs would be sold in the coming three-day period, quoting the packer as authority for the statement. The American people take pride in their hot dogs—presumably because they are so American. Editors, knowing this, used the story, giving credit to the packer, on many front pages.

We could go on with the story of Bill and hundreds of other Bills and Marys who have worked on newspapers or other publications, and eventually entered public relations work. Training in journalism often serves as an internship for a public relations career.

Being long-established, journalism has done much for the stability and knowledge and technical skills of public relations, which is still young as a field of activity.

Just as the public relations field has benefited from the lessons that journalism and allied fields have to offer, this same excellent journalistic training of many public relations workers has in turn helped the press, which receives from them facts and ideas, properly interpreted in usable form. Most newspaper staffs would need sizable expansion if it were not for material prepared in public relations offices.

However, with a great oversupply of publicity for the editors to sort out, they throw away material which has no news value or other interest for their readers. They discard a badly written story (in rare cases they might rewrite it). They don't use releases which violate principles and practices of journalism. They recognize the value of the work of a public relations practitioner with good journalistic training or knowledge, who uses judgment in the selection of what he writes and puts it into proper form.

Of course, work on a newspaper lays a valuable foundation for careers in various other fields. In saying this we fully recognize that a great many top-notch workers should continue in journalism, to fulfill the important missions of that calling.

Working for magazines provides some experiences different from newspapers. While there is some overlapping, each field gives excellent training for a public relations career.

The transition from getting a diploma to doing public relations work seldom takes a direct route. Usually a preparatory period intervenes, frequently in journalism, but sometimes in selling, advertising, printing, business-paper editing, or broadcasting. Some prominent public relations counselors or directors first trained as engineers, lawyers, teachers, or personnel specialists. Some of the leading women public relations practitioners started in business as typists or stenographers.

In Review

A summary of some of the chief lessons of journalism for use in public relations follows:

1. Development of ease in interviewing persons of all kinds.
2. Understanding of individuals and groups in order to win quick cooperation in getting to the point.
3. Accuracy in details and in overall impression given to readers.
4. Presenting the gist in headlines and opening paragraphs.
5. Sharpening of memory and gaining knowledge of how to get information quickly on almost any subject.
6. Contact with many phases of human activity.
7. Promptness—meeting deadlines.
8. No excuses for failure to carry through an assignment.
9. Use of correct grammar, punctuation, capitalization, and building a readable style.

10. Increased vocabulary and proficiency in semantics.
11. Control of own emotions in trying to understand other persons; development of objectivity.
12. Finding out successful policies and practices in dealing with public opinion.
13. Avoidance of fiction in statements intended to be factual.
14. Not overplaying an insignificant or mediocre story. However, an element of novelty or unusual human interest might be uncovered which would justify extensive treatment.
15. Editorial work on magazines as well as newspapers gives good training for public relations.
16. Other aids are found in selling, advertising, graphic arts, and broadcasting.
17. Public relations personnel comes from many other fields, but study of journalism is especially helpful.
18. Journalism benefits public relations, and public relations personnel with adequate knowledge of journalism render service to all media of communication.

•   •   •

We now begin to work up an appetite for searching out the heart of a complicated problem and how to solve it.

CHAPTER IV } The Five "W's"

O NLY AFTER A PERSON gets an insight into what public relations means in toto, and after he acquires some basic
information about various subjects pertaining to human relations
should he start to study a formula for solving a problem in this
area.

One counselor, in approaching almost any new problem, usually says to his associates, "Well, let's make a survey."

He does not necessarily mean to hire an opinion research firm,
although that step often should be taken. What he does mean is
"Let's learn the essential facts and opinions on which to base our
deductions and recommendations."

In carrying out this thought, he has found that knowing how
to interview key persons is the initial step.

* * *

Mr. White, the chief executive officer of a machinery business,
invites a public relations consultant to explore a problem which
has come up unexpectedly and on which the practitioner has had
little advance information.

In dealing with a complex public relations problem and the
project which may come later, the consultant will find it highly
desirable to have a basic working formula. This will change somewhat for each situation, because no two are exactly alike. Nevertheless such a general formula offers valuable and necessary
guide-posts.

Some of the public relations workers say that "they play by

ear," or "throw the book away" in approaching each new set of conditions. Actually, each inclines to operate with procedures which have turned out successfully.

Let us assume that you are the public relations counsel whose services have just been employed by Mr. White.

As a first step in the formula, you get him and others in the corporation whom you interview later to tell you about the problem as each person comprehends it. You will need to ask many questions.

•   •   •

Borrowing from newspaper experience, you cover, in your interviews and research, the five W's—what, who, when, where, and why.

What?

The "what" question usually should be the most thorough because it grapples with what Mr. White and his associates regard as the general problem, as well as the detailed phases of it.

What the fundamental problem really is often varies from what those who are close to it think it is. For instance, the head of a cosmetics company had created the fine idea of starting to train executives and other personnel for a whole generation ahead, as well as keeping the present staff "on its toes."

He put so much emphasis on the future that he neglected the present. Bright young men and women came into the organization with enthusiasm, expecting to become high-salaried vice presidents, or at least department heads. Many of the young people were soon disillusioned and they resigned. Some felt that the management lived in a dream world concerning some far-off time. Others looked on the future planning project as merely a publicity device.

The head of the company believed that the turnover of talented employes stemmed from some of his vice presidents' ineptitude. Actually, the lack of balance between current operations and long-range planning caused the trouble.

Who?

The "who" covers the attitudes of Mr. White himself; others with whom you will need to work in his organization, and the publics involved.

Your first public centers in the one person, or small group, dominating a situation. If you cannot correctly comprehend and win this public you are lost. You must win enlightened, enthusiastic backing from this inside public if you get its cooperation in several vital ways, such as giving you the full information you need, having confidence in your analysis of the problem, and taking your advice on how to solve it.

One counselor in dealing with a new client usually makes it a practice at an early stage to conduct a thorough study of what the top echelon of management thinks about major matters that have a bearing on his work. He also checks with the secondary echelon of management—and its views usually differ somewhat. They exert immediate influence on their seniors and some day several of today's juniors will inherit the authority of management.

The word "who" should bring into focus the publics to be understood and influenced.

On one occasion, a company may think it should try to influence the general public, whereas a limited group of influential opinion molders suffices.

In another situation, the public generally should be the prime target, and specialized groups should be secondary.

Careful analysis will point the way to the right answers.

When?

"When" brings up the question of historical background and the timing of the project upon which you work—whether for a short period or for long duration.

As an example of a rather quick solution of a public relations problem, take the planning of a celebration of an organization's anniversary. An oil company in marking its 75th year in business publicized its progress in the past. To get the background facts required a great deal of study. But it mainly emphasized the 75 years ahead. In doing so, it announced plans for building a huge research laboratory. It awarded college scholarships to several high school seniors—sons and daughters of employes—with the implication that they might serve the company in the future.

To the general public the stress was on new and improved products then going on the market—with strong hints that still better products would follow later on.

To mention another angle on timing, some public relations counselors miscalculate the intentions of a new client. He might have made up his mind firmly to use public relations services for a limited period on one specific project, whereas the counselors might assume that he should and would continue for a long period with a complete program in mind.

The problem of timing comes up constantly in such matters as the hour of the day for a news deadline, the best days of the week for an announcement, the right season of the year for launching some new project, and the time needed for preparing people's minds for an important change.

Where?

"Where" may involve your asking Mr. White such questions as these: In what cities does he operate plants and offices which are to be considered? Where does he distribute? Are the sources of his supplies in the picture and, if so, where are those sources?

Another manufacturer, in the electric products industry, with plants in many parts of the United States and Canada develops a training course on economic education for his employes. This course requires serious mental concentration in order to be highly effective.

So the consultant, using his knowledge of cycles, mentioned in Chapter II, suggests zoning the training courses by various latitudes. In a band running fairly straight, East and West, from New York through Chicago, intellectual interest generally reaches a peak as Winter changes to Spring. In Canada this point comes a little earlier, in Southern United States, somewhat later. (This example, of course, involves an overlap of "where" and "when.")

· · ·

Many public relations programs need to be reviewed for factors of geography and topography. Mountains, fertile farm regions, arid country, industrial centers, and sea coasts create special problems.

Why?

"Why" calls for the causes leading up to the general subject which Mr. White has brought up for discussion, and reasons behind each important phase of it.

In covering a news story about a fire, a reporter learns to find out, if he can, why it started. Also in trying to comprehend a problem in public relations, a practitioner needs to know why that "fire" started.

Sometimes this can be fairly well unraveled by interviews with a few well-informed individuals; or by studying records and reports, and reading between the lines. Frequently, you may need an expertly conducted opinion survey to get a diagram of reasons underlying a difficult problem.

In a rather isolated large city, with unusually keen civic pride, the leading local industrial company merges with a larger company headquartered in New York City. The local company, now a subsidiary, retains its name and most of its old management personnel. Relations with the community and the city and state governments continue affably. But the parent corporation becomes an aloof absentee landlord. Also it changes the name of its subsidiary and arranges for the popular local top executive to leave on pension in advance of his normal retirement age.

On the surface little or no initial reaction to the changes comes to light. But soon the tax assessments increase. A city ordinance is passed which looks somewhat discriminatory to the company. At a jury trial in which the subsidiary is involved because of a serious accident, the organization fares badly. Government inspectors become more strict. Two senators and a congressman may have a hand in that.

Then comes a long spell of serious labor trouble. The management blames it upon the labor union. Actually, a public relations analyst finds that this surface reason does not disclose other fundamental reasons.

As a result of his advice, the old name of the company is restored. The able and respected former president returns, as a management consultant, from his premature retirement. He does this enthusiastically. A well-rounded program in all phases of human relations is planned and put into effect to deserve and win the good will of the employes and the people of the city, with its octopus arms reaching city hall, the state government, and, to some extent, Capitol Hill in Washington.

In Review

"What" covers the nature of a problem as seen through the eyes of those closest to it, including facts and opinions with a bearing on the problem.

"Who" gets into the subject of the individuals for whom you work and the publics you want to influence.

"When" involves historical background and timing.

"Where" brings up facts about geography—location of places of business, distribution outlets, and sources of supply.

"Why" calls for reasons leading up to the current problem.

A good newspaper reporter wastes no time in most interviews. The same applies to a public relations worker. The five "W's"— what, who, when, where, and why—you can remember easily, and they cover a tremendous amount of territory.

CHAPTER V } Four Main Parts of Life

IN ADDITION TO USING the what, who, when, where, and why of newsdom, there is another simple formula helpful in interviewing and other preliminary research. It originated with an idea developed many years ago by the Young Men's Christian Association.

That organization set out to encourage a sound mind in a sound body, plus strong spiritual power. Later, it added to this trinity the concept of good social values—as getting along well with other people and having fun. These ideas cover a great deal of ground in human relations—most of it, in fact.

With some stretching and overlapping, you can make effective use of the mind, spirit, body, and society formula in approaching a human relations problem through interviewing and research.

The Mind

A public relations counsel must build a bridge between an individual leader, or management of an organization, and the publics involved. The foundations begin with the person or controlling group. Otherwise you couldn't even start the bridge. There would be neither dollars nor moral support for its construction.

So, you must understand your sponsor's thinking. In one management, in the hardware business, four men, as a team, had control. Each had a large financial interest, successful experience, and a high regard for the opinions and sensitivities of the other three.

Three of them wanted to take some courageous, progressive steps in their relations with employes, plant communities, dealers, suppliers, customers, and the public generally, but the fourth demurred. Policies of several years ago had worked well, and he hated to see anything new attempted. The public relations specialist received a warm reception from the three executives, and he thought the majority would rule.

However, he made the serious mistake of not working sufficiently with the fourth member. Such an effort might not have succeeded, but it should have been attempted. The specialist failed to comprehend the thoughts and attitudes of the one person essential for a favorable decision of the group as a whole.

This experience is offset by happier results in many other instances. Sometimes a board chairman, company president, or association executive-secretary possesses so much power and ingenuity that he overcomes all opposition. At other times, the thinking of several individuals must be studied and correlated. In any case, the key person or persons should be understood from the outset.

·   ·   ·

On some occasions you find an important executive grossly misinformed or uninformed on some phases of human relations. He may wrongly take for granted the love and respect of employes or customers or residents of his community.

His enterprise in general may succeed because of an advanced research, sales, or production department. Or it may have exclusive patents or advantages in sources of raw materials. Hence the executive may assume that he excels on all fronts.

One such executive, at a huge evening rally in a civic auditorium, was asked by a sycophantic announcer, during an intermission, to rise under the spotlight's glare and take a bow. Instead of the thunderclap of applause which he expected, a barrage of booing burst forth.

Until then, he had almost totally misinterpreted local public opinion. Study of public attitudes revealed several fundamental errors he had made unwittingly. The public thought of him as having harmed some of the popular interests of his city. Actually, the executive had quietly done many worthy things for the city, and he had good motives—unfortunately hidden in a tower of thick ivory so far as the public was concerned.

This extreme example shows how far away from the facts of life an important person, highly proficient in other ways, can stray in the field of human relations.

On the other hand, some executives, with little training in public relations, develop an uncanny knack for grasping its meaning and how to use its power.

•   •   •

The president of one company, when it was quite small, said that he knew what his employes thought. The office and factory had a large washroom for the men. The only thing he needed to do to learn the men's opinions, he said, was to get in a closed stall in the washroom for a few moments and "keep his ears open."

His successor, now with thousands of employes, knows that such attitude "studies" are of little value. And he knows that people disapprove of such methods. He depends on scientific kinds of opinion research.

The mental or intellectual phases of a public relations problem bring up many pegs on which to hang useful questions in your research. For example, you need to learn how a management communicates with its publics and how it gets information in reverse flow—both are highly important on the two-way avenue of public relations.

We have barely touched upon the mental phases of a situation. But if you remember the Mind-Spirit-Body-Society formula, recall of each of these words will cause lights to flash on the control board and help you think quickly of appropriate questions in a well-arranged pattern.

The Spirit

Man represents an astounding hodgepodge of mud and stars. Concerned about his health, his job, his house and car, and hundreds of physical or material things, he darts back and forth between them and spiritual considerations. Often they become fused or confused. As a well-rounded person, a man or woman needs a balance among mental, spiritual, and material forces, along with social consciousness.

In the battles of the mind in a public controversy, a strictly materialistic appeal usually doesn't work unless tied to something on a higher plane. Huey Long did not use a slogan such as "Let's all get rich." He refined it to "Every Man a King," which to many signified both wealth and benevolent authority—and a release from feelings of inferiority.

A rich suburban community in New England faced the prospect of a huge superhighway through some of its choicest residential districts. This would mean the roar, vibration, and smell of trucks all day and night, disturbing a strip at least a mile wide through the suburb. Also, hundreds of fine homes would have to be razed. The basic reason which caused the citizens to organize and fight the proposed highway was frankly one of self-protection or self-interest. This might be called materialistic, but reasons on a higher plane began to emerge.

To defend one's home and neighborhood seems only natural and desirable. The beauty and spirit of a fine community would be largely destroyed by the highway. Recreational facilities, a boys' club, churches, and schools would be affected adversely. A cheaper alternate route would do less harm and still meet traffic needs. So, a public relations campaign combined spiritual and intellectual appeals along with the materialistic.

Something similar applies to the individual or management group controlling an organization. Any reasonably normal person harbors spiritual urges. In the preliminary stages of working on a public relations problem, you need to detect these urges.

In one corporation only one consideration showed on the surface—making every possible cent of profit, without much thought of possible harmful side effects. Making a profit is commendable and necessary. But still greater profits can be—and are—made by managements which have a genuine interest in their employes, plant communities, stockholders, and customers. The management which thinks *only* of profit and thereby ignores human beings gets into serious trouble sooner or later.

A successful enterprise of long standing renders some worthy service or it wouldn't be where it is. Therefore, it has within its activities something that could be interpreted as a creed or perhaps the basis for a crusade. Public relations skills should formulate and dramatize such ideas. Sometimes this knowledge emerges in early interviews and research, but usually it takes considerable time.

On one occasion, the president of a drug company in his first interview with a newly employed consultant clarified several of his management's basic spiritual and other objectives. For instance, he said he wanted his employes, their families and friends, and the customers and other publics of the company to become aware of his organization as an unusually good employer. At the same time, he wanted all these publics to realize that his company conducted an all-out campaign for the relief of human suffering, the saving and prolonging of life. With such truthful concepts set up, there should be still greater acceptance for the quality and value of his products, already widely recognized.

Members of the management of a food products corporation worked out a kind of spiritual theme: "We receive more only by giving more." The company quickly passed along to the public many of the savings from increased efficiency and production. Employes and stockholders also shared. Profit on each item dropped, but the grand total of earnings on greatly increased sales mounted appreciably.

Two leading manufacturers in a heavy goods industry offer another example. The management of the second-largest company determined to surpass its rival. While this could hardly be thought of as a spiritual force, a situation did develop into what could be called a crusade among the senior and junior executives. To reach their goal they realized at the outset that they must *earn* their leadership by designing and producing superior products, giving customers a price advantage, and rendering better service. After nearly 10 years, they finally attained industry leadership. Then the effort shifted into *maintaining* the number one position by constantly *deserving* it.

Most managements have within themselves the makings of a theme on a high plane. But usually they have not clearly recognized it. Perhaps they live too close to their work or just don't realize the importance of a high level theme. Public relations workers should ferret out such things and put them to work.

During World War II, millions of farmers and factory and office workers sincerely wanted to do something extra to win the war by aiding their relatives and friends and other young people in military service. Nearly all factories did some kind of work directly or indirectly supporting the war effort. This set up a spiritual or emotional force for many persons doing rather hum-drum jobs. But by the time of V-J Day a natural let-down fol-lowed.

Much of this spiritual force can be replaced. Many enterprises produce equipment which should make this country and its friends more secure against Communist aggression. Others pro-duce drugs which save countless persons from pain and death. Even the simple aim of one company to provide greater cleanli-ness in the home, when explained clearly to employes and cus-tomers, fires its activities with greater meaning and lifts it out of strictly material channels.

As early as you can, in exploring a public relations problem, look for spiritual values around which to rally all other forces. A nation's flag at the head of a parade inspires in that it symbolizes love for one's country and its welfare. Likewise a public relations program can receive a great lift, power, and significance through the right kind of theme and symbol.

Sometimes an idea of this kind is developed and made widely known, but not entirely lived up to. An organization must carry out its stated aims, otherwise it creates ill will.

In interviews and research, when you think of "spiritual" in your check list, other questions may come to mind. For instance, is religion a factor, as it often is in a complex human relations problem? In one factory most of the employes belong to churches, divided rather equally between two sects. Each of these two churches has vitality and good management. They have influence in various public relations situations relating to personnel and the community.

Sometimes it takes a great deal of digging to explore spiritual factors that have a bearing on a problem and you may not get the answers in the preliminary stages. But it pays to try, and you may discover a beautiful white horse to head your parade.

The Body

By "body" we mean "physical" and "material," in our check list for covering initial ground in talks with well-informed people and in exploring records, as an approach to a public relations problem.

For instance, consider age and physical condition of an executive group. Management needs a combination of youthful spirit plus good judgment, aided by long experience. The president of a university, with a board of trustees numbering 20 besides himself, says that he knows fairly well in advance how they will vote on any issue involving a rather progressive, new step. Ten probably will favor it—they are the younger men and a few of the older ones young in their outlook. The other ten, mostly old in years, have grown cautious and want the organization to conserve what it has and take no unnecessary chances. The president, after carefully weighing both viewpoints, often casts the deciding vote.

In understanding a management group, a public relations worker needs keen insight into facts about age and health as they affect attitudes of members of top managements.

You can easily err, however, if you regard the oldest man in the group as reactionary. Sometimes a youngish executive is a "stuffed shirt," while his septuagenarian chief retains the mental fire of his thirties.

One of today's most successful advertising agents, in starting his business many years ago, needed a short-term loan of a few hundred thousand dollars. Contracts from clients covered the risk. He talked to a bank vice president, with no encouragement. Then, with knocking knees, the advertising man entered the walnut-paneled office of the bank's president—a wizened gnome of 80 years. After hearing the advertising man's story, the president smiled heartily, said it looked like a fine investment, and why hadn't his associate granted the loan sooner.

Older men have more experience and usually more objectivity and sound judgment than younger men who, if unchecked, might occasionally take ruinous chances. On the other hand, in some management groups a few men approaching retirement age, losing all hope of further advancement, sit out their last few years as executives more or less trying to keep out of trouble, taking no risks of losing what they and the enterprise have.

A public relations worker is not hired by the public, even though he works in the public's interest. A group leader or a management committee employs him. To get your airplane off the ground, you must get your gas and clearance papers from your sponsors. To do that you must understand them well and earn their confidence.

•   •   •

While on the subject of health we might mention briefly something about the current trend among corporations to arrange for thorough medical check-ups for executives.

These examinations bring forth some surprising information. Some executives find their hearts so weakened that they must slow down to keep alive. They naturally worry about their condition and this often affects their attitudes and their work.

In the case of one company, a public relations consultant discovered considerable unrest among the first and second string executives because of their organization's system of medical check-ups. These officials, scattered in a dozen cities, had to go to a hospital in a certain city at specified times for check-ups by a specialist who unfortunately had an unpleasant personality.

The executives favored dealing with their own family physicians or specialists instead of the stranger. The specialist gave his full reports only to the president of the company. The executives felt that such reports should be personal and confidential. After getting the doctor's analyses they thought that it was up to them as individuals to take proper action.

This is a controversial subject. The executive with chief responsibility believes he should know the physical condition of each important subordinate, so that he may intelligently plan or adjust the duties of an ailing person. He could help the situation by selecting specialists in several cities, convenient for executives. They probably could develop cordial relations with their new patients. Family doctors also could continue to serve, except for the yearly check-up, and they might be called in for consultation.

·   ·   ·

Many questions come under the heading of "physical."

For instance, take sex and age. In one fairly new manufacturing company, many employes are women—mostly girls recently graduated from high school. The large turnover hinges on marriages, boredom, and restlessness.

In another, older, organization in the stationery business, most of the workers are elderly men and women with long service records. Such "physical" facts need to be learned in some phases of public relations work.

In studying an employe and community situation, look into housing—also schools, churches, playgrounds, amusements, and transportation. In some communities, industrial pollution of the air has a seriously depressing effect on the people—physical as well as mental and emotional.

Bad surroundings in a factory or office have a harmful impact on many workers as well as on visitors and the community.

Mr. North, a wholesaler, was amazed when his employes went on strike. Later on, he called in a counsel to assist him and his personnel director. Among other steps, he started a program of better housekeeping. As new painting was needed, he chose cheerful colors. Washrooms were tidied and brightened, and many little hazards to safety and health removed. Employes showed their appreciation on their faces and in their work.

Customers who came to visit complimented Mr. North and other members of the management. The improved appearance pleased the neighborhood.

Creature comforts or discomforts and pleasant or unpleasant appearances can do much to help or hurt human relations.

·   ·   ·

In this chapter we have touched on physical aspects of human beings. For purposes of a check list we also include under the term "body" other material things, such as products.

You may advise occasionally on how to use public relations knowledge and techniques in introducing a new product.

Mr. West, during World War II, worked with a group of scientists on some military projects. He saw that several ideas with which he dealt could be adapted after the war to highly useful civilian products in the consumer goods field.

The first item he introduced succeeded dramatically in early tests. So, he wanted to follow up promptly with five or six other ideas he had in mind.

Public relations counsel suggested to Mr. West that he concentrate on his first product and establish national distribution with great public acceptance for his brand before competitors got ahead of him—the old army idea of getting there "fustest with the mostest."

After Mr. West attained this goal, he began to add the other new products, one at a time. He now had the organization and financial backing to proceed safely and soundly.

·   ·   ·

A company frequently may request your ideas for promoting a new or improved branded item.

There are countless ways to do this kind of job, some of which will be described later. Techniques used for many years may still prove effective. But you need to add some novel elements in order to stand out.

The reporting of a survey of public opinion often results in widespread publicity for a product or a cause. But to be news-worthy it must have an element of freshness or timeliness.

At a time when headlines gave the impression that teen-agers, in vast numbers, had become dope addicts, one company announced a study of habits and thoughts of representative young people in all sections of the United States. This survey clearly indicated that most young people are wholesome in what they think and do. The press and radio gladly reported the details, with credit to the sponsor of the study.

We have mentioned only a few of the images conjured up by the words "physical" and "material." Each problem brings forth its own indigenous questions.

Most Americans may resent being called "materialistic", especially by citizens of other nations. Probably people of other nations inherently are as materialistic as we are, but most of them have failed to show *results* comparable with America's.

While Americans have many fine spiritual qualities, it is true that they have raced far ahead of others in the material field. Our successes have been so vast that they have created an economic imbalance in the world, with repercussions in many directions. If America even stirs in its sleep, it causes nightmares for many other nations in their economy and politics. With six per cent of the estimated world population, the United States creates more than half of the world's production and services in many fields.

Society

Having a sound mind in a sound body is highly desirable, as the practitioners of psychosomatic medicine have proved, and many of them recognize that it is essential to have strong spiritual power geared in.

The human being wants to have fun, recreation, entertainment. And he has a primary need of adjusting himself in his relations to other individuals, to special groups, and to society generally.

Therefore, in dealing with a public relations problem, we must consider these basic facets of life.

●   ●   ●

In one isolated community, where a large company owned nearly all the land and buildings, the management knew that its troubles with its employes and the community resulted from several factors, but it overlooked some of the most important ones.

There was no motion picture theater within several miles of the center of the community. The nearest public playground and amusement park were even more remote. Schools and churches were shabby and cramped. Dilapidated shacks mingled with company-owned houses. Occupants felt little sense of responsibility toward the houses they did not own.

The river, once full of game fish, had turned black with pollution. Frequently the air smogged the residents and fly ash dirtied washings on clotheslines. Even on Saturday nights when, in most other places, large numbers of adults "step out," 19 out of 20 of them stayed at home. Television had not yet reached the community.

Cultural events, such as concerts and lectures, were among the missing. Only the labor union hall and the factories showed their lights far into the night. Adequate parking space was lacking around the factory buildings. Shrubbery, if any ever had been planted, apparently could not stand up against the fumes.

All these conditions, depressing to human beings, apparently existed unnoticed by the management.

The little children of the neighborhood looked as bright and handsome as those of any more fortunate community. But many of the older children and their parents looked beaten-down or bewildered or resentful.

Luckily for everyone, the absentee owners of the local plants took to heart the results of an independent study of this community and started on a long-range program to correct the abuses.

•   •   •

One industrial group in a large city realized that many of its troubles sprang from the city's slums. Most of the slum dwellers had no indoor toilets—no playgrounds for the children—insufficient garbage collection—no high-grade cultural or entertainment facilities close at hand. If you have not inspected an alley in a real slum, it would be a shocking experience to wade through the knee-deep debris.

Many city ordinances on the books called for proper housing and living conditions, but public sentiment had not been roused enough to cause proper enforcement.

Without any new municipal legislation, public opinion was worked up by a group of public-spirited organizations, through publicity and speeches, to a point where a broad swath of the slums was cleaned up. Outdoor toilets disappeared with the installation of indoor plumbing. Buildings were painted and repaired. In the center of each large city block a concrete-floored playground appeared—hosed off periodically by city employes.

On one side of a thoroughfare, the old slums still stand in their depression and filth. On the other side, the inhabitants seem so proud of the improvements that they have lined the sidewalks with potted shrubbery and flowers. They show more care with their personal grooming, they stand more erectly, and they smile.

Along with material improvements, this experiment has added cultural and recreational advantages. Business has benefited and so have the families and the community.

* * *

Another aspect of social relationships can be found in the hostess plan of selling of which Stanley Home Products has become the leader. A housewife gives a party for 5 to 10 or more women. A dealer will demonstrate products, conduct games, give prizes, sell merchandise, and conclude by signing up one or two of the guests to arrange other similar parties at their homes. Many hostesses repeat their parties.

The hostess usually serves coffee, cakes, cookies, and other refreshments. She puts her home into immaculate condition.

Why does this happen? Most people want social contacts. Many of them are fairly new in their community. Or they have been too poor or too busy for social activities. Or they want to establish their own friendships—not merely retaining those of their parents or other relatives.

These may seem intangible forces, but they are as strong as steel. They have helped create scores of flourishing businesses and rendered a real service.

In Review

You need to learn about the knowledge and thinking of a management and its publics—what they know and don't know and what may be misconceptions.

Spiritual factors often enter a public relations problem and a project for its solution. People need and like sublimation of earthy issues. In business, large profits often coincide with managements most considerate of other people. Every successful enterprise of long standing has within itself the makings of a creed with a spiritual quality. Public relations has a responsibility to locate and crystallize such credos in an enterprise—also to discover and meet the higher kinds of yearnings of the public.

Physical factors concerning a management and its publics should be noted. More and more attention is being given to health in America and this gets unusual emphasis among executives under the heaviest nervous tensions. Age and sex of employes have a bearing on personnel relations, and so do physical surroundings.

Under the general heading of "body," both physical and material questions come to mind. Material things include products, because a great deal of public relations work involves selling of things, as well as ideas.

The cravings of the human being for satisfactory social relations seem universal, although they often are frustrated, especially in disorganized or deteriorated communities. This may happen in run-down towns or in city slums. The urge of the housewife for pleasant social contacts is demonstrated in the party system of selling which has swept the country.

So, in interviewing and other researching, take a keen look into the social aspects of a human relations problem.

They round out the mind, spirit, and body line-up and cover some of the major phases of human life.

·   ·   ·

In interviewing and other research leading up to understanding and solving a public relations problem, one of the easiest and most widely inclusive check lists to carry around in your head is Mind, Spirit, Body, and Society.

CHAPTER VI { **All Business Is Divided**
{ **Into Several Parts**

ENERAL MANAGEMENT is one of the greatest of all arts. We
gaze reverently at a painting by a genius who has interpreted his own deep emotions and thoughts or those of a group
or an epoch. We listen in awe or rapture to compositions of an
inspired musician.

But few realize the consummate art, as well as training and
skill, needed for one person to coordinate and harmonize the
conflicting interests of dozens of divisions and departments
and thousands of individuals within a large enterprise. He also
must adjust contradictory demands from outside his organization.

On the inside, investors want more dividends, while labor demands more pay and benefits. Externally, suppliers desire higher
prices but consumers want to pay less. Government meanwhile
piles on heavier taxes. It adds up to so much confusion and con-
tradiction that many a major executive has wondered why he
should bother with all the trouble involved in trying to solve the
mysteries of the labyrinth. He is not fully satisfied with his decisions. He merely arrives at the fairest, most practicable balances
he can.

He gets well paid, as he should. The demand for outstanding
general managers is large and the supply small. The few who
excel often work longer hours and put more mental and nervous
energy into their jobs than almost any employe down the line.
The chief executives sacrifice much—time with their families and
friends, recreation, cultural pursuits, and their health.

Why does the chief executive officer of a large organization continue his strenuous routine, even after he has all the money he needs for the rest of his life and enough for his heirs? Perhaps he just enjoys his work. Or he feels he renders a public service. Or he doesn't want to "let his organization down." He is only human and gets a thrill from a feeling of power and prestige. He may have wakened to the fact that he is a consummate artist in the field of human relationships—getting thousands of individuals to team together. In a sense, he seems like a justice of a court in making difficult decisions. In any case, rarely do you find such a leader driven only by the urge of monetary gain.

In dealing with the top commander of an organization and his principal aides, public relations practitioners must appreciate such background considerations. This leads to another rather simple but vital check list in analyzing and solving a complicated problem in human or public relations.

Knowing that the high command in an organization must understand and coordinate several major functions, interests, and activities, the public relations executive or consultant should turn a searchlight in those directions.

The Idea, Product, or Service

The Patent Office at Washington bulges with plans and working models never utilized. Some of these seem uproariously funny. Some look clumsy, picayune, or dull.

Others make so much sense that you wonder why they haven't been put to use long ago. Here is why they haven't. It takes too much money, education, effort, and time to break down consumer, investor, and trade resistance to many of the available new ideas, products, or services.

For example, look at quick-frozen foods. In the 1920's, when investors learned of the idea, it sounded plausible. Investors risked more than 20 million dollars as a starter, gambling on what might or might not turn out a successful enterprise.

The facts of life often are cruel and exacting, as they were in this case. The public confused quick-frozen foods, full of good flavor and other values, with cold-storage foods some of which have less flavor and lose certain nutritional values.

Suitable storage equipment was lacking for shipping and storing foods at below-freezing temperatures. Grocery and meat stores had few or no facilities for this latter purpose. The cost of the early storage cabinets was almost prohibitive, especially during the early stages of a terrific business depression.

Physicians, nutrition experts, and home economists—guardians of public health—had to be convinced, as they should be—of the merits of the strong claims made for quick-frozen foods.

Much of the investment world stared with a stony eye at the whole project, with more millions of dollars recorded in red ink.

But the sponsors persisted, making improvements in product research and processing. Experts gradually became convinced of the nutritional merits, the sanitary qualities, the freedom from waste, aid to suppliers, and convenience and time-saving for housewives.

Then came lower-cost equipment which could be rented or bought on easy terms. Suitable production and distribution were created. An avalanche of public education began to break down consumer resistance. Finally, earnings' reports showed black instead of red and a new industry boom rushed ahead with giant strides.

Nearly a generation has passed by in the meantime. There probably would be no quick-frozen foods in large volume today had it not been for this expensive and laborious process. Some simpler, new ideas take hold much more quickly, but for each success the wrecks of failures litter business history.

This illustration shows the need for far-sighted statesmanship in management and the fact that public relations and publicity form part of the warp and woof of complex industry and business. Promotional aspects must hold hands with a sensible idea, research, finance, supply, production, and distribution, as well as with human factors of patience, ingenuity, and ceaseless effort in order to attain success.

So another check list takes shape for the preliminaries required to bore down through varied strata before striking oil. The several basic classifications to be checked cannot fall into any exact order because they overlap and intertwine. The first fundamental, of course, is an idea or ideas which make sense from the standpoint of public interest and probable ultimate business success, as illustrated by the story of quick-frozen foods. The other areas to explore begin with management.

Management

You can hardly stress too much your comprehension of the management of an organization. When almost the entire policy rests in one person, you may find that his judgments on vital questions are sometimes influenced greatly by his wife, a friend outside the business, some old-time, trusted employe, a chance acquaintance in a Pullman smoker, or a chauffeur.

For instance, one company president in the transportation field had employed a radio star to spearhead his company's promotion. The actor's listenership ballooned, as did the company's sales. But the president's wife loved classical music and at her insistence the actor's services ended. The actor's next sponsor increased sales by 300 per cent in a short period and continued at a high level.

This extraordinary example shows how a chief executive's decisions may combine strong impacts from various sources.

•   •   •

Absolute monarchs have just about disappeared from the Western World, but a few of them still remain in business. In some corporations a chairman of the board, president, or principal stockholder usually has his way. Sometimes he represents a family or group with financial control. Or through ability and hard work, he climbs to the helm and stays there. The trend, however, definitely favors *group* management.

Whatever the make-up of a management, a public relations counselor must size it up promptly and correctly. One public relations counselor for several publicly-owned corporations, each with thousands of stockholders, undertook the job of advising a family-controlled company. He almost immediately got into difficulties because he tried to apply what he previously had learned to a kind of management different in various ways. Publicly-owned companies usually frown upon nepotism. But in family-owned companies, very different problems arise regarding relatives of the controlling family.

Mr. Southern, the only son and heir of the founder and owner of a successful home appliances company, has five sons who will inherit the control some day. They will have responsibilities to thousands of employes, several communities, many dealers, and customers. They ought to know a great deal about the enterprise which they will control. To get such knowledge they should *work* for the company—learn by doing.

Therefore, Mr. Southern explains to his sons the desirability of them taking jobs in the company, if they some day are to do an intelligent job of making important decisions. So far as possible the young men must earn their advancement from the ranks. They must not stand in the way of progress of talented employes who deserve promotions. To Mr. Southern the idea of inducing his heirs to grow up in his company in this manner is not nepotism. To him it means common sense—in fact, almost a necessity.

There are about as many different kinds of management groups as there are individual executives. Variations in the individuals alter the patterns. To comprehend these patterns is often essential in understanding a public relations problem, and especially in working out a sound solution which the management group will support.

Where the Money Comes From

Along with a good idea for a product or service, and with a competent management, an enterprise must have sound finances. Many public relations workers, trained in journalism, advertising, teaching, or personnel administration, have slight knowledge of the financial problems of a corporation. Wherever this shortcoming occurs, it should be corrected by sharpened alertness.

One public relations adviser for a medium-sized chemical company early in World War II formulated a long range program—for at least 10 years. The management believed its greatest single problem centered in the field of employe relations. The adviser recognized the importance of this viewpoint, but stated his belief that the greatest need would be capital for expansion. The field in which the company operated had great potentials. The management was capable and alert, its products excellent, and its research well abreast of the field.

The analysis turned out correctly, and gradually the management recognized it. The chief executives, close to immediate problems such as employe relations, had paid little heed to the approaching needs for repeated new financing for expansion.

As a result of their new understanding, the company built a well-rounded program of investor relations, which included better financial reporting in pamphlets and in the press. Interesting stockholder meetings were held. Security analysts, investment counselors, bankers, and financial editors received useful information, visited the company's plants and research laboratories, and became acquainted with the management. A friendly letter and background literature greeted new stockholders.

You can find other important techniques in stockholder relations. But a public relations worker needs to know more than the methods. He should figure out essential interests of the people involved.

One industrial company decided to set up a large contingency reserve—a proper thing to do under the circumstances. But the management planned to deduct the entire amount covering a year's period in a single quarterly earnings statement. This would show an unprecedented drop in the company's profit for a three month period. The quarterly earnings for many years had stayed on a fairly even keel. The sudden drop would cause consternation among many conservative investors in the company. It would worry some of the employes, distributors, plant communities, and other publics. Then, three months later, the earnings would show a big jump back to around normal. This would create confusion, and possibly even suspicion of manipulation, in the minds of interested persons.

Therefore, the public relations officer of the company urged that setting up reserves be spread over a longer period. Also, he advised, the reasons for the reserves and the manner in which it was done should be intelligently explained.

The management wanted to do the right thing, but it had not looked ahead to explore the probable misunderstandings that would have resulted.

In public relations, you must not only do what is honest and fair, but also you must see to it that you are not misinterpreted.

One enthusiastic public relations executive, strong on ideas for publicity and weak on knowledge of the financial limitations of his employer, advocated a series of projects. These would have attracted a great deal of attention for the company, but they would have wrecked a sales and advertising program essential to the welfare of the business. Much of the money for the proposed publicity projects would have to be withdrawn from the sales and advertising budgets.

"I can dream, can't I?" asks the publicity man.

Surely you can and should dream. But let's open both eyes and walk around this dream, and see where the money is coming from or where it might be in the offing, and what is likely to happen if it is taken away from some of the organization's other major functions.

In public relations, one must learn the *wholeness* of an enterprise and *interrelationships* of its various functions. Financial considerations rank high on the check list for study of an organization.

Sell to Survive

An egg is fertilized. That compares with the inception of an idea or a product. Then management must keep the impregnated egg alive and flourishing during its early, as well as its later, development. There must be wherewithal or nourishment from the outset as well as continuously thereafter. That phase might be compared to finance. Other functions appear almost simultaneously. One of them is *sales*.

Even in a family of young poultry or barnyard animals, some "runts" cannot "sell" or protect themselves adequately. While they get the abuse, others step forward into leadership.

In the broadest sense, every human being needs to do a certain amount of selling to survive, whether in business and trade, in charities or colleges, or in everyday living.

The public relations worker must have some understanding of the product or service, competition, pricing, and markets. For example: For many years two corporations battled for first place in selling coffee. In trying to outdo each other they tried new public appeals. Some succeeded; others failed.

A public relations counsel made an objective, long-range study of public reactions to the appeals by the two companies. One of the findings stood out: For expensive coffee, the most productive approaches to the public in fairly normal times consist of good flavor, enjoyment, and glamorous or emotional appeals which enhance the taste, aroma, and pleasure of certain brands. Price reductions, new types of containers, and research achievements have helped, but usually in a secondary way. Novel types of promotion get results, especially when they carry out the concepts of superior flavor, pleasure, and other factors which contribute to those ideas.

Another way to stimulate sales of many products comes from the constant injection of *news*—improvements, new uses, new values, new models, and new ideas.

As part of a check list in your effort to find the core of a problem and its solution, the subject of sales may prove most significant.

Advertising Can Pay

Company B had progressed far in nearly all aspects of its human relationships. A public relations counsel listened to this directive: "While we think we act progressively on nearly all fronts, a sketchy public opinion study portrays us as less popular than some of our competitors. The study gave no reasons for the public attitudes. Please see if you can locate our weakness."

After checking the product, management, financing, and sales organization, all of which seemed to be excellent, he ran into something about the advertising which revealed clues to the trouble.

In a rather frantic effort to overtake the popularity of competitors, Company B's advertising executives had resorted to exaggerated claims. The public will stand for some exaggeration in advertising. But public opinion revolts against anyone stretching the truth too far. In case of Company B's product, thousands of people had begun to single out its advertising as a bad example.

One school of thought preaches you can intentionally irritate the public greatly and get top billing in sales through using overwhelming promotion. This idea may work in certain instances for a limited period. But it is a hazardous concept. The public has more intelligence than some people seem to think. In spite of abuses in a rather small percentage of advertising campaigns, the standards today have risen higher than those of a generation or two ago during advertising's adolescence. Also the ethics of business generally have risen appreciably since the beginning of the century and most people have come to expect to have this fact demonstrated in sales and advertising practices.

The president of C Company asked a public relations consultant to look at an advertising exhibit in a conference room. Along one side he had displayed his own company's advertisements for the past year—on the opposite wall the advertisements of a more successful competitor.

"We have what we consider an advertising agency and an advertising department second to none," the president remarked. "We engage the best of copy writers and commercial artists. Yet our studies show that our competitor's advertising has registered with the public far better than ours. Just look at our ads individually! They seem to stack up favorably."

The president put his finger on the trouble with the word "individually." His competitor had concentrated for years on building up a single important impression about itself in relation to the public, and in terms of the public's interest. Company C's advertising rambled "all over the lot," covering many apparently unrelated ideas, spreading confusion instead of depicting a definite, favorable image in the minds of customers. Company C had several powerful and opinionated executives. Each promoted some pet idea he wanted in the advertising. But the overall effect, in spite of the beautiful layouts and copy, reminded the counselor of a kaleidoscope.

The conclusion, of course, was that the advertising experts should get acceptance of a definite theme and program and gain protection from undue interference in carrying out their jobs.

Public opinion studies regarding advertising show that most people think of advertising generally as a fine and useful thing for themselves personally and for our economy and society. But the public criticizes chiefly these three things in advertising:

1. Untruthfulness (exaggeration, crowding the truth, unfair use of words).
2. Bad taste in all forms, either in illustration, headlines, or copy appeals.
3. Attacking a competitor. People don't seem to mind if you "blow your own horn" a little, but they don't want you to go out of your way to harm other folks who try to render a service and make an honest living.

• • •

Public relations, in the opinion of some scholars, encompasses all human relationships of an organization. Publicity, these scholars state, comprises the promotional phase of public relations, or the communication of promotional ideas, which include advertising. But these definitions have lost touch with the reality of common usage.

Today, to most practitioners, public relations affects nearly *all* human relationships. In industrial relations, for example, a public relations worker can contribute something regarding psychology of employer-employe relationships and especially in the communications between the two groups. But industrial relations has become a highly developed field in itself.

Publicity, as referred to in this book, does not mean advertising. Publicity reaches editors, commentators, and other opinion molders, to be accepted or rejected, edited or rewritten, and used at the time the editor sees fit—if at all.

Advertising is paid for at a definite rate, to be used in a specific form, almost always at a scheduled time. An advertising medium may refuse to accept the advertising or request a change in it, but this happens rarely in case of reputable advertisers.

Public relations specialists often are consulted or have direction of so-called "institutional advertising," or "public relations advertising," designed to promote an industry, an organization, or an idea, rather than specific products or services.

Sometimes you may find a public relations advertising campaign the best solution to a complicated problem. The information you wish to get to the public is not interesting enough for editors to feature sufficiently—or quickly enough—to get the public to understand your message. But with powerful, interesting advertisements you can establish your ideas—sometimes rapidly.

Advertising, publicity, and public relations activities do not compete. They should operate together in harmonious ways. When a housewife sees an advertisement about a new type of synthetic detergent, then reads a favorable editorial by a woman's editor, followed by some evidence of public interest on the part of the manufacturer of the product, she is likely to be considerably impressed.

Sometimes a high grade advertising campaign is hurt by unfavorable publicity resulting from bad public relations policies of a company management. On the other hand a company with generally good public relations and publicity may be injured by advertising which strives too hard or is off-color in some way.

Some corporations or organizations buy little or no advertising. For example, one company supplies a complex type of engine and other equipment to a single customer, or to a very few. However, several hundred of the largest American corporations advertise nationally. Many thousands of others advertise in limited localities or areas. So, in studying a public relations problem, the subject of advertising frequently arises.

Production Interests People

In the United States and a few other countries, mechanization has advanced on a giant scale. From childhood, most people in these lands find fascination in machinery and production of mechanical things. Therefore, the manufacturing angles of a corporation or an industry stand out in the study of many public relations problems.

A medium-sized food specialty company almost went broke because a zealous production manager, trying to save money for the enterprise, made what seemed to him a slight change in the production routine. But the consumers didn't like the results at all. They didn't complain—they just stopped buying the product.

Company D, in the paper industry, ran into trouble with its publics because it announced in enthusiastic terms a new item which thousands of persons eagerly wished to buy. But the manufacturing end of the business miscalculated and could not deliver in any suitable quantity for more than a year. This resulted in antagonisms among distributors, dealers, and many customers. Editors, assured of the product's availability by the time they announced it, received disapproving letters from readers. So the editors turn their pique against the manufacturer.

In some exceptional cases, the announcement of a forthcoming product should break well ahead of quantity production. In the field of medicine, a new discovery usually is reported promptly in the scientific press, even though supplies of the essential materials are extremely scarce. In the interim, preceding mass manufacturing, clinicians can experiment further and familiarize themselves with proper dosage and treatment, with limited available supplies. Chemists and engineers have time to improve production methods. Then, later on with ample supplies on hand, the public benefits because of this period of experimentation.

In case of a whole new concept for an industry, educational work may precede by years the widespread availability of the products—for instance, nylon and quick-frozen foods. The public needed to become pre-sold on the revolutionary ideas it learned would materialize eventually.

Company E made medicinals of high quality in rather large quantity. It wanted its customers to think of this merchandise in terms of quality. But its publicity emphasized the size of the factories and large number of employes. A study among its customers showed that they had the impression that Company E must have slipped somehow in its quality standards because of publicity about mass production.

The subject of production comes up in many forms in a public relations study and often should rank rather high on your check list.

You Buy before You Sell

Certain raw foods grow only in limited areas and sell largely through cooperative marketing services. Some ores are mined by only a few companies. Other raw material supplies are highly centralized or limited in some way or other, even without government controls.

Therefore, some critical public relations problems center around suppliers, and, in times of national emergencies, the cooperation of governmental officials.

Especially in times of shortages, the good will of nearly all suppliers assists a corporation. A certain supplier normally sells to 10 or 12 large outlets. The demand is acute and his available supplies reduced. He tries to dole out whatever he has available on an equitable basis. One outlet gave him a hard time consistently when he really needed the business. Another has been considerate with him at all times. Both buyers ask the supplier to adjust his allotments in their favor. If he decided to favor either of them, it is obvious which he would choose.

Some far-sighted organizations cultivate the good will of suppliers at all times. They know it pays. The president of a large company in the metallurgical field spends some time each year calling on his suppliers as well as customers, including some rather small ones. A one-time little supplier grew large. Then came a period of acute shortage. He did everything possible to take good care of the company whose president had once visited briefly with him years before.

High officials can't spend much of their time visiting thousands of suppliers. But, through their good will building policies and practices, they can cement fruitful relationships.

·   ·   ·

Mr. Abbott, general manager of a food company, foresaw shortages and higher prices. He stockpiled one commodity so heavily that it appeared he had "cornered the market."

His public relations counselor pointed out the dangers, such as repercussions from the government which then had a war on its hands. Members of Congress and officials in Washington would demand an investigation. The press would print exposés, harmful to practically every activity of the company and to industry generally.

The counselor recommended several immediate steps:

1. Begin to sell gradually all of the supplies not actually needed. To unload suddenly would break the market and harm many people.
2. Inform any interested part of government that supplies would be available to any company which really needed them.
3. Notify commodity exchanges of this fact.
4. Intensify research already started which gave promise of a development in the commodity which would relieve a serious shortage in another field.
5. Make a statement of these facts to the press.

All of these steps and several others were taken promptly, and prevented what might have been serious trouble.

Public relations should have been in the picture prior to the mistake. This applies to supply problems and all other major phases of management.

Either Modern Research or "Else"

Most people seem fascinated with scientific research; so, a public relations worker may find highly useful material in that phase of his study.

Numerous companies today derive a large part of their sales and income from types of products not in existence 10 to 15 years ago—such as antibiotic "wonder" drugs, synthetic detergents, new kinds of plastics, and electrical equipment. Without research for new and better ideas, methods, products, and services most enterprises might as well liquidate.

A public relations worker should know well in advance about

any forthcoming new or improved product, so that he can plan effectively. In addition to news releases, he may find it advisable to prepare booklets and background data, photos and charts, and perhaps a motion picture. The announcement may call for a meeting with the press.

Mr. Burns, chairman of the board of a manufacturing company, asked for public relations advice on a new machine of a highly complicated nature. The public relations counselor wanted to know whether the machine would cause trouble when not handled by an expert operator.

Another public relations problem was that the invention would throw many people out of work. The exterior of the machine looked ugly and an industrial designer was needed to make its appearance attractive. Thousands of people would see it in operation.

The counselor asked for a demonstration. The machinery promptly broke down and skilled mechanics worked several days before it ran again.

So, Mr. Burns held up on any announcement for several months, until he became convinced that the invention was really foolproof. A designer streamlined the exterior of the machine. He then installed the machines gradually in cities with the highest employment.

•   •   •

Company F spent millions of dollars in research on a mechanical product—to make it in a less expensive way. By the time the research ended, competitors had learned how to reduce costs even more drastically than Company F, and F suffered a setback. This displeased stockholders. However, later research by the company more than offset the loss, and after explanation of this fact, stockholders became satisfied.

Research always has an element of risk. After great effort and investment, a new idea develops only perhaps to become outmoded by some better competitive work. But, without research, many companies would lag far in the rear in the competitive race.

Research symbolizes progress, growth, and strength. Properly interpreted in public relations work, the subject of research offers opportunity for building good will.

• • •

Research in the field of opinions furnishes one of the chief tools of public relations. Skillfully applied, it takes much of the guesswork out of defining human attitudes, misinformation, and knowledge or the lack of it.

Opinion research often helps to find the heart of a problem and clues to its solution. A later chapter is devoted to this subject.

Another form of research in business has to do with markets. In America's highly competitive business, management should discern quickly any signs of significant changes or new trends.

In the promotion of a certain brand of food, a new radio program was started. It quickly won the public's favor and sales in retail stores boomed. But the pipe lines between retailers, jobbers, and manufacturer had been full and orders at the factory did not immediately reflect what happened. In fact, a competitor, at that time not alert in his market research, did not fully wake up to the changed competitive situation for several months.

Varied Functions

Each organization being different, major functions vary. One company employs hundreds of engineers while another needs none. One concern is international in scope and another confines its dealings within a single state. But a business or industrial corporation's check list of functions usually runs fairly long. Included are governmental relations; tax, patent, and legal; relations in other countries; traffic; insurance; engineering; problems of health and safety, and various other human relations.

Most companies face numerous governmental problems—city, state, and national, and sometimes international. At Washington, thousands of public relations practitioners work in governmental activities, or for companies, associations, and other organizations in almost every field. Public relations men from large cities all over the country visit Washington on special occasions.

Suppose you are assisting an industrial association which has been asked to provide testimony at public hearings held by a committee of the House of Representatives. You must learn the procedure involved, what led up to the hearings. Your association leaders will want your help in planning some prepared statements to be read at the hearings. Numerous copies of these should be reproduced at least a day in advance of a hearing before a Congressional committee for the committee and for distribution to the press. In addition to these releases, you should anticipate as much as possible probable questions and proper answers.

The United States government has mushroomed into the largest activity in the world. It affects every individual business, in some cases so extensively that a corporation must maintain a Washington office with personnel to handle relationships with government departments and bureaus. Some of this work involves public relations, so your check list of functions should include government—at all levels.

On the legal front, a public relations worker can't expect to know much about the law but he must learn to work closely with lawyers. This need grows as new laws pile up every year and as managements become more aware of public opinion. Cooperation between legal experts and public relations people has increased. Both viewpoints should be, and often are, represented at important policy meetings of management. An important statement prepared by a public relations department often requires a careful check-up by a lawyer. Vice versa, a release written in precise legal language usually can read more effectively if it has the benefit of public relations treatment. A clear, readable, persuasive announcement can be written soundly from both the legal and public relations' viewpoints.

Regarding export, a public relations worker trained in the United States, has problems which on the surface seem almost insurmountable. The differences in language and idiom can be largely dissolved by competent translators. But the variations from country to country in history, culture, folklore, and national aspirations are so great that no one man or woman can expect to comprehend more than a small part of them. So, specialists must be relied upon.

One general guide for good public relations in other countries is to observe basic facts about human nature which are universal. A clue to this fact is found in *Reader's Digest* studies which show that its articles of greatest interest in the United States rate high with readers in other countries.

Traffic is another item on your check list of functions. It may be strictly local, involving transportation of employes and visitors to and from a place of business, parking facilities and regulations, bus stops, or highway overpasses or underpasses. On a national scale the good will and cooperation of the transportation field is highly desirable, not only because of the need for the best possible services but also because millions of transportation workers and their families form a huge market.

Several other functions of a large business organization might need exploring in your interviews and other research. But we will confine the remainder of this chapter largely to human relationships.

Human Relationships Provide a Key

Most problems encompass the field of human relationships. For example, Company G, a jobber, suffered from a long, bitter, expensive strike. The industrial relations director, heavily burdened with many tasks, could not devote sufficient time to communications between the management and the employes. So a counseling firm, experienced in that specialty, assisted him.

An attitude study, made in every department, showed up the few big sources of the trouble as well as many little ones.

The industrial relations department developed a comprehensive program to remedy many things. The counseling firm proceeded to write explanations of the program for the employes step by step, as the program unfolded.

Within a year marked improvement in the relationships of employer and employes became apparent.

•　　　•　　　•

Mr. Caldwell, head of a home appliance company, with its employes on strike, told his counselor, "When this strike ends, I want our employes and their families to like and respect the company more than ever, as a result of our conduct and of what we say and don't say."

Local advertising and news releases were written from the standpoint that the company tried to work out the fairest possible solution for its best friends—its employes. With no note of bitterness or innuendo, the various issues were stated clearly.

Letters sent to the employes' homes explained new points raised in the labor negotiations. The company went to great lengths to notify employes about maintaining certain company benefits, such as insurance and use of the company's recreational facilities.

Several months after the strike a study of the employes' attitudes toward the company showed that they couldn't have risen much higher at any time.

The Neighbors

A chemical manufacturer wanted more popularity for his company in his community. He thought of a dozen reasons why he had not attained his goal. Finally, he came to the core of the problem. As he told a friend, "the people think we stink." By that he referred to the foul odors from his factory. The abatement of air pollution was the principal thing the local public cared about.

Once he realized the gist of the problem, there were two major steps to take:

1. Some definite action which would tend to reduce ill will and create good will.
2. Inform the public so as to get the action understood and appreciated.

Adopting this platform, the chemical company executive:

1. Made a careful study about abatement of air pollution for his plant and then did all he could to reduce the odors.
2. Kept the public informed, both about the study and about the corrective measures. In this case, the gradual abatement of the odors gave dramatic proof of the validity of the manufacturer's intentions and efforts.

At a meeting of the Public Relations Society of America, in Chicago, in November, 1951, some novel suggestions came to light for handling a problem of this type.

For instance, one idea included the slogan, "Sell That Smell." A Mid-West manufacturer was urged by a U. S. Government agency to rush to completion a factory to manufacture supplies to United Nations' forces in Korea. The factory would exude unpleasant though not harmful fumes. It could not get equipment for abatement of the nuisance. So the management explained these facts to the public before the factory went into operation and stressed the point that whenever a resident noticed the odors he should recall that they meant urgently-wanted aid for our armies, as well as wealth and growth for the local community. Apparently this line of reasoning appealed to the neighborhood around the plant.

Good public relations implies responsibility for correction of abuses. If the correction requires a long-range program, explain this clearly to the public. If correction looks temporarily impossible, this also should be explained.

Those Who Take the Risk

Human relationships in publicly-owned companies include those with stockholders. They take the risk with their investment, but they are human beings first and stockholders second. When they buy stock, most of them enjoy receiving a letter and booklet from the company. They like readable type, interesting copy, and a pleasing format.

When they write to the company, they expect to receive a friendly, prompt, clearcut reply. And when they attend a stockholders' meeting, they enjoy a cordial atmosphere. In some cases, stockholders have a sizable impact on a company's business, especially when the management suggests in a gracious way to stockholders how they can help build good will and sales.

Also, stockholders can cause difficulties, in case of a proxy battle and participation in stormy annual or special meetings, resulting in bad publicity about some unpopular management policy or practice concerning investors.

By and large, however, stockholder relations offer an opportunity for constructive, long-range building of understanding and good will. This makes new financing easier and helps build sales and a good reputation.

Your Dealers

One public relations counselor, in discussing various human relationships, asked his manufacturer-client to tell him about the attitudes of dealers who sold his products.

"Oh, the dealers' attitudes don't count," said the manufacturer. "Our products have such public demand that the dealer *must* handle them. So we don't do anything especially to cultivate dealer good will."

A study soon afterward showed that the dealers actually had a sizable bearing on the company's sales. Interviews with a cross section of retailers brought to light the fact that many of them resented the company's attitude and recommended sales of competing products whenever suitable occasions arose.

As a result, the manufacturer reversed his earlier stand and tried to deserve and win the support of dealers.

Molders of Opinions

A few thousand men and women alter the thinking and feeling of millions.

One editor or broadcaster alone may influence great masses of people regarding what foods to eat, what clothes to wear, what to think about certain organizations or industries, political issues, and many other subjects.

Nearly every home in the United States has one or more radio sets. And now television enters the picture, affecting the attitudes of people and the way they vote and spend their time and money.

School teachers influence children who, in turn, carry ideas into the homes, thus reaching the minds of parents. Social workers, having considerable influence in their own right, say that the channeling of thoughts through school children to adults in the home exerts a powerful and beneficial force.

The clergy, both through sermons and personal interviews, have profound impacts on public opinion. So do lecturers, labor leaders, doctors, lawyers, pharmacists, salesmen, and others who talk to many people. Active officers of organizations of all kinds, ranging from national associations and professional societies to local Parent-Teacher groups, help to shape the public's thoughts.

Barbers, operators of beauty parlors, taxicab drivers, and many kinds of business people transmit information and thought which help to mold the sum total of public opinion.

Key public opinion molders now include thousands of public relations practitioners.

We have mentioned only a few of the molders of opinion. More and more recognition goes to the desirability of enlisting the help of these persons in public relations programs.

Nearly every problem presents a special line-up of such persons worth cultivating. For instance, Company H erected a new office building. It made an effort to explain to policemen and taxicab drivers the location of the building and the street with the most desirable entrance. At the same time, it hoped to inspire some friendly comments about the company.

Company I, with a new food product, informed nutrition experts, physicians, writers on food subjects, home economists, and food distributors and dealers before launching advertising and publicity to consumers.

Time published a cover story about Dewitt and Lila Wallace and the *Reader's Digest*, Dec. 10, 1951. The story powerfully depicts the influence of leading opinion molders on the public. *Time,* itself a great force in this field, stated, in part:

"No one can measure the influence the *Digest* has had on its readers, but it has certainly been considerable. It has also had a marked influence on other U. S. magazines—and through them, on the U. S. education. Thanks largely to the *Digest's* successful example, nonfiction articles now play a dominant role in U. S. magazines. Thus Wallace has lured many people to read about serious topics, and in this sense, has helped raise the reading level of America.

"He may even succeed in getting more Americans to read books—in abridged form. Recently he started publishing quarterly books, each consisting of four or five outstanding books, predominantly fiction, condensed into a single volume. The last one sold 460,000 copies, much greater than the usual sale of a Book-of-the-Month-Club book.

"In the long run, Wallace's greatest contribution to the nation may be found in the cumulative effect of his overseas editions. Invariably, his readership surveys show that articles which U. S. readers like rate equally high with readers everywhere. The *Digest's* articles—depicting the innate decency, kindness and simple virtues of ordinary Americans, the triumphs of a George Carver or a Helen Keller—have probably done more than all the Government propagandists combined to allay the fears, prejudices and misconceptions of the U. S. in other lands. As one French *Digest* fan said last week: 'We have discovered that Americans are just like other people.'

"Insofar as they are 'just like other people,' the *Digest* is doing a worldwide educational job of telling the truth about Americans. Is it the whole truth? The *Digest* tells the world that Americans are optimists who believe that happiness, as well as success, can not only be pursued but captured.

"If the whole truth is deeper and more difficult, the *Digest* has no concern with that."

In Review

A check list of subjects to be explored in interviewing and research in a large business organization includes:

1. The basic idea, product, or service.
2. Facts regarding the management.
3. The principal financial factors.
4. Selling, advertising, and publicity.
5. Production.
6. Purchasing.
7. Research—scientific, opinion, and market.
8. Human relations—with employes, communities, stockholders, dealers, and opinion molders.
9. Government relations, law, patents, trade marks, taxes, export, insurance, and traffic.

It may seem laborious to peer into all these avenues. In many instances, you must make decisions so quickly that you lack time to do a thorough exploratory job. But with time not at a premium, it pays to look at every major facet of a business.

In that way you get a better understanding of each part of the corporate body and how it fits together. Tucked away in some inconspicuous spot you may discover clues to the true nature of the public relations problem and its solution.

CHAPTER VII } How to Handle Background Reading

I N ADDITION to interviewing well-posted persons who can throw light on a public relations problem, a good deal of reading comes into the picture—before, concurrently, or after your interviews—probably a combination of all three.

Incidentally, while conducting your research, several ideas will take tentative form for subsequent strategy, theming, and devices.

In your reading, you should employ about the same yardsticks or check lists suggested for interviewing:

1. The list worshiped by many newspaper reporters—the questions, "what, who, when, where, and why."
2. The formula consisting of mind, spirit, body, and society.
3. Questions based upon major functions and activities of an organization—management, finance, marketing, personnel, stockholders, etc.

You may develop a set of questions of your own to cover a wide assortment to be sure you overlook no angle of possible importance, such as analysis of your publics by age, sex, locality, occupation, income, education, and group organizations and interests. But on most occasions select simple check lists you can carry in your head without referring to notes. Therefore, we suggest the three fairly simple groups of questions.

You may be overwhelmed by the material for reading. Therefore, select carefully. For example, suppose you struggle with a public relations problem raised by the removal of a factory from Connecticut to New Jersey.

In the case of such a limited problem, your study would concentrate largely on what happens to the employes and their families and the two communities. What information and services should you explore? What about sufficient advance notice of the move, data on housing, schools, transportation, etc.?

Here you would waste valuable time and effort if you minutely examined every phase of the business. But you can fruitfully beam check-list questions at restricted phases of the business.

For instance, "when" brings up the timing. If possible, a year's advance notice should be given because of employes' leases on homes or apartments.

"Who" reminds you to learn all you need to know about the employes and communities in question and just how they will be affected.

"Why" calls to mind the need for careful explanation of the reasons for moving the plant.

In case of the removal of a factory from an upstate New York town, "before and after" surveys showed that the company actually gained in good will as the result of wise explanations and other steps taken in the program. The citizenry became convinced that the move was economically necessary and that every reasonable consideration was shown to employes, their families, and the town as a whole.

The check list of mental, material, and social elements could be applied in a special problem like the shifting of a factory. And some ideas could come to light by running through the list of major functions of the business which might be involved.

Skim-Reading

Learn skim-reading, because of the overpowering volume of printed material to analyze. With practice, a person can speed-up his reading and still grasp essential information. Some passages may prove worth reading several times, others hardly rating a glance.

Some lawyers and editors become so adept at skim-reading that whole paragraphs or pages seem to be photographed in their heads. A public relations worker once showed copy for a 32-page booklet to Mr. Darlington, a corporation lawyer, who thumbed through the pages rapidly. Then, without referring to the copy he commented that pages 11, 17, 22, and 29 required some slight changes because of legal reasons. The public relations man, amazed that a person could read anything so fast and remember it, asked about points on several other pages and found that Mr. Darlington recalled the contents accurately.

Few people can duplicate this, but most public relations workers can save precious time by intelligent skimming.

On one occasion, a public relations worker, to meet a deadline, skim-read more than 1,000 pages of the Congressional Record and other material over a weekend. By Monday morning he had grasped enough of the essential information to help in defining a complicated problem and offering suggestions for its solution.

Other Aids

Developing a strong memory is a plus in public relations, as it is in journalism and other fields. To have a good memory usually calls for a powerful *desire*. A corollary is the *energy* to follow up the desire. Also, helpful techniques abound.

As an aid for remembering names after you meet a person, one device you can use is to imagine a photograph of the person with his name printed on his forehead or neck. Another method is to ask the person to repeat his name or even to spell it out, if somewhat unusual. Thus hearing and seeing combine forces.

Still another method is to think of some association of the person's name. Suppose you meet a man named Edwards and you elect to associate with him the thought that several Edwards reigned as kings of England.

In addition to remembering persons, places, and various facts, public relations practitioners should know where and how to find a wide variety of information.

A corporation official receives a letter from a charity asking for a large sum of money. On the surface the request looks worthy but the official knows nothing about the charity and has no record of it in his files. He asks a public relations worker for comment.

Several channels present themselves for arriving at the answers, depending upon the charity's nature, or locale. One source may be a Better Business Bureau. Or, someone may call in person; write for fruther information; or, check with some contributor who knows about the subject. Some companies build up large files of their own regarding organizations which seek money for donations or memberships.

A public relations department or counseling firm should have numerous reference sources. Also the personnel should have know-how about the services of a public library; how to get a copy of a radio script, biographies of persons in foreign countries, or, a correct quotation. A chapter entitled, "Public Relations Tools and Media," in the book, *Your Public Relations*, spells out principal reference sources.

Some organizations find it worth while to hire a digester of books, magazine articles, reports, and long letters.

Mr. Farrington's desk accumulates papers, many of them originating from within his company. He sees the pile growing; and more material coming from outside his organization. He cannot keep up with his work unless one or more skilled persons prepare for him some brief digests, outlining the gist of the material, both from within as well as from outside the company.

A national news magazine's researchers wrote 85,000 words

about a single subject. Then digesters cut it down, and a writer put it into final form with about 5,600 words. Sometimes a digest edits down to a single sheet.

One excellent public relations research man recalls Cotton Mather, who, when jogging along on his horse, would write notes on a variety of topics and pin them on his clothes. On returning home he would sort out the notes into an orderly pattern for his sermons. His modern counterpart does not ride a horse, but he makes innumerable notes on index cards while he does his research. Then he arranges the cards by subject matter and finds the process helpful in devising a logical pattern for his material. Orderly arrangement of thoughts earns high rewards in public relations work.

Let's review another suggestion for studying background material—"read between the lines".

A letter, memorandum, or report may conceivably show up on the front pages of newspapers some day. Or the material may get into unfriendly competitive hands or cause trouble in some other way. Therefore, a great deal of business writing emerges cautiously, and a research worker learns to interpret the words and ideas. For instance, a memorandum may indicate an undercurrent of worry about some problem, although the words look reassuring on the surface.

Confidential minutes of meetings of important committees often give the researcher guideposts for understanding a problem.

In Review

To sum up the points about background reading:

1. Use approximately the same simple check lists suggested for interviewing to examine each approach.
2. Be selective in reading, especially with an assignment in a

limited area, such as the problem of removal of a factory. But, even here, broad check lists may help.

3. Learn to skim-read and to cover large amounts of material quickly, still getting essentials.

4. Develop memory by strong desire and energy to follow through with various techniques.

5. Learn where and how to find answers to questions—quickly and correctly.

6. In large projects, have a skilled person digest the vast amount of material involved.

7. Learn to "read between the lines" and interpret cautiously written statements. Minutes of meetings often aid in getting an accurate viewpoint.

CHAPTER VIII } Learning What People Really Think

MANY PUBLIC RELATIONS problems have been identified and solved without the aid of formal opinion research surveys. Some emergencies come to a head so suddenly that you lack time for such studies. Certain managements hesitate to spend money for surveys, either because they don't realize what they miss or because they think they know enough of the facts already, as indeed they sometimes do.

The field of opinion research has grown up rapidly as many executives have come to recognize its values. The worthwhileness has shown up clearly time after time in defining a problem and in getting clues for its solution.

Dr. Claude Robinson, president, Opinion Research Corporation, writes in a chapter in *Your Public Relations*:

"Ordinarily, at the heart of any problem involving public psychology are one or two major ideas. These ideas are usually crucial to sound public relations strategy. If the public relations man knows them and builds his campaign around them, he gets results. If he is right on his fundamental strategy, he can be wrong on day-to-day tactics and still get results. If he is wrong on his fundamental strategy, however, even brilliant day-to-day tactics will fail to get results.

"The first contribution of research to public relations then is to furnish a reliable photograph of public opinion which enables the public relations man to define his problem and map out the strategy of his campaign. With objective data in hand, the public relations man can then go to his superiors and get agreement on the course of action to be followed and secure the budget necessary to carry on the campaign."

Understanding of Employes

The president of Company J, with several hundred employes, stated that he had a clear insight into their thinking and attitudes and didn't need to have a modern personnel department. A public relations consultant made a wager with the president that the latter would find himself in error about his employes' attitudes if he conducted an opinion study.

This intrigued the president and he authorized such a survey. Later, he was shocked at how little he had known about what the men and women around him really thought. He promptly improved his personnel department and launched a program designed to correct abuses and to build understanding and good will.

•   •   •

Mr. Gordon, general manager of a public utility company in the Mid-West, accepted an offer of a similar job in the East. He suspected that the morale of the employes in the Eastern company was low and he decided to explore that problem. Opinion research showed morale even lower than he had thought. Also, the study indicated *why* it was low.

While there was little complaint about wages and salaries, there was widespread ill feeling against the previous management which had given employes too little information and had not bothered to learn about or to correct misunderstandings. In fact, many employes indicated they would have been skeptical of anything the former management might have said.

Working conditions were unsatisfactory. Supervisors had little or no training. Some employes were ashamed to tell anyone where they worked because of the ill will of the public. This ill will affected not only employes but also the attitudes of customers and city and state authorities.

Mr. Gordon and his public relations counselor hammered out a program. It emphasized the idea of "the new broom" in all its human relationships. People tend to give a new man a chance to show what he can do before criticizing him.

Numerous internal abuses were cleaned up and informational programs started. The public heard repeatedly of reforms and improvements through advertising, publicity, and speeches. After 12 months of these activities, a study among customers and the community at large showed sweeping gains.

• • •

Company K, from time to time, suffered severe unrest among its employes. Its mills would slow down or close due to strikes, and customers placed orders with Company K's competitors, at least temporarily. Employes and the community were hurt badly. At such times the management would decide to do something drastic.

A competent director of industrial relations joined the company on one of these occasions, but the management failed to support his program and he soon resigned. By that time the mills operated full blast again and consideration of sound employe-employer relations was largely forgotten.

Later, during another work stoppage, the managers went into a huddle and decided that an outstanding opinion research company should report in great detail about the roots of the trouble. The study brought out facts and opinions which the president, the principal stockholder of the company, didn't believe. He mulled over the findings for several weeks, but by that time the employes went back to work. (It is rare that such a study is made during a strike.)

The cycle of "boom and bust" in labor relations encored. The management decided that the opinion research report had become out-of-date and some new palliative should be applied. A young man recently out of college was brought in to act as director of industrial relations. Bright and earnest, but inexperienced, he could not successfully cope with the problem. A public relations firm, with a long and successful record in counseling in such situations was engaged, but was told to confine its efforts strictly to selling the community on the management's views.

The main point of this story, happily an uncommon example, is that there is no value in competent opinion research, industrial relations, and public relations services, unless they are followed up with suitable action.

•   •   •

Mr. Hardy, president of a distributing company, pursued an opposite course from that of the head of Company K. After his employes, for the first time in history, walked away from their jobs, he engaged a consultant.

He accepted his counsel's suggestion of a complete opinion audit among employes several weeks after the strike. The counsel received assurance from Mr. Hardy that, after the findings of the audit had been conscientiously studied, steps would be taken to remedy the most important things which seemed to be wrong.

The audit brought out some surprising things—some of them more pleasant than Mr. Hardy anticipated. But others disappointed him. Mr. Hardy realized that the employes knew what they were talking about when expressing their personal attitudes, and that he couldn't have known what was going on in the heads and hearts of hundreds of different individuals unless they told him through a survey conducted with anonymity.

An opinion audit almost always boosts morale. Some employes say, "I have worked here for 20 years and this is the first time my advice has been asked for. I like the management's attitude in this and hope that the opinions of some of us will be taken seriously. I'll give the boss the benefit of the doubt and wait and see what happens."

Mr. Hardy made sure that some flagrant abuses, of which he had not been fully aware, were cleaned up quickly. Employes saw constructive things happening. Mr. Hardy wrote an occasional letter to the employes at their home addresses and explained improvements already in effect or under way. The families and friends of employes learned the news and were pleased, to the extent that they urged some of their friends to apply for jobs at the company. This was at a time when the company had difficulty in recruiting suitable new employes.

Mr. Hardy sent letters to employes at their home addresses to explain results of the opinion audit. He told them which of their suggestions could be accepted promptly, those which would take a longer period to put into effect, and some which were beyond the financial power of the company to adopt.

Industrial relations experts advise that a management usually should make major improvements one—or at least a very few—at a time and make sure they are properly installed and thoroughly understood. Too many big changes in a short time cause confusion. So, Mr. Hardy instituted only a few major changes plus numerous minor ones in the first year after the opinion audit.

The effect of the program was noticeable to nearly everyone working for the company or doing business with it. When employes feel they are part of a team with management in a worthy cause, it influences the ways in which they and their families and friends talk to other people. The change shows up not only in employes' conversations and personal contacts, but also in promptness and accuracy in filling orders, and in services beyond the call of duty.

An opinion audit of employes wastes time and money if not

followed up. On the other hand, prompt and adequate follow-up reaps an excellent harvest.

•   •   •

The public relations director of a household products company tells a story of what good public relations among employes can do.

The P. R. director took a seat in a coach of a featured train of a railroad which had wakened to the value of public relations, had studied employe and customer opinions, and had inspired its workers to cooperate in a program of building good will. The conductor and a trainman smiled and made some appropriate and cordial remarks. A trainman reminded the passenger that he would be welcome in the club car at no extra charge, if he wished to sit there.

In the dining car the passenger experienced new thrills in the promptness, efficiency, and friendliness of the waiters. At a hotel (allied with the railroad), where he attended a convention, a waiter, also trained in public relations, spoke to the guest by his correct name, Mr. Ingram. The guest suddenly realized that the waiter had merely used his eyes and looked at the place card in front of Mr. Ingram. Nevertheless, he appreciated the attention.

On his return home, on the same train, Mr. Ingram was amazed and delighted that the conductor and trainman remembered him and commented that they enjoyed having him join them on their return trip. Also two waiters in the dining car said the same thing.

Such experiences are exceptional, and Mr. Ingram completed his trip with the following thoughts:

1. Conviction that employes with proper training and inspiration multiply favorable impressions with the public. Any

employe of an organization can and should be an effective salesman.

2. Determination to extol the merits of this particular railroad and its sound public relations on every suitable occasion.

These are reasons why this incident appears in this book.

Knowing a Community

An employe in a factory or an office may spend 40 hours a week on his job, with the remaining 128 hours devoted to other interests, including, perhaps, 56 hours of sleep. Thus, much more than half his waking time is not at his place of work. The individual is first of all a human being—a citizen—and secondarily an employe. So, an employer of workers should understand their interests and attitudes as persons. If he employs many people, he should know what the community as a whole thinks about him and his enterprise—the community having a direct bearing on his business in many ways.

If well thought of locally, he attracts many of the ablest candidates for jobs. If families and friends of his employes admire his company, they use their influence to recruit new workers and to reduce labor turnover. They buy and promote the company's products or services.

There are some intangibles in determining tax assessments and if any favorable breaks can be given they tend to go to enterprises most highly regarded in the community. Juries reflect public opinion and so do civic officials. The running of a large company mixes with countless community relationships, especially in medium-sized or small cities where a large enterprise has high visibility.

Company L was one of eight large employers in a circle of communities with a 5-mile diameter. The company expanded rapidly and needed a constant influx of new workers. Most of the jobs called for more than average intelligence and aptitude to acquire technical skills.

In addition to recruiting, the company had many other local problems. City officials often seemed to be uncooperative, for instance, in traffic situations. Various local groups campaigned spasmodically against the company's pollution of air and water.

Company L decided to hire an opinion research firm. A map of the area was laid out so that the neighborhoods chosen for interviews were representative. The interviewers did not know that the survey was being made for Company L. They were asked to show each interviewee a card with the names of the eight leading local companies, and then learn how they ranked from various standpoints.

A pilot study of 50 interviews indicated whether the questions were clearly understood or brought out useful information. The wording was revised slightly. Some questions were dropped and others added. With the improved questionnaire, the interviewers called at several hundred homes.

The tabulations showed Company L generally regarded with favor, but several interesting exceptions came to light. There seemed to be little feeling of warmth or enthusiasm regarding Company L, in contrast with one or two other organizations. Management of Company L was considered a good employer but somewhat aloof and not wholeheartedly interested in community welfare.

The community knew of stream and air pollution but did not blame any one company for the bulk of it. In fact, considerable confusion showed up on this subject. On another point, some residents near the factory believed fires broke out almost continuously in the plant's buildings, because of the factory's system of using bells which rang loudly to call certain supervisors to the telephone.

After studying the survey, Company L decided to make the community better-informed. It held a successful open house, with many thousands of the local residents trooping through the factory and office buildings with obvious pleasure and interest. Other open house events, with new forms of exhibits and entertainment, will follow. A comprehensive visitors' program welcomes as many as 100 or more persons daily. An attractive booklet is given to each person. News and photographs as well as advertising are sent to local papers.

Specialists have been assigned to community relations assignments. One supervises the effort to abate air and stream pollution. Another keeps close contact with opinion leaders and influential organizations in the area. Still another heads up educational work through the printed word and through speeches. Careful study of contributions and memberships shows whether the company fulfills its local obligations properly.

Through all these techniques the company tries to make it clear that it has a feeling of warm friendliness and a genuine interest in the welfare of the community and all the people in it. Without the opinion study the company would not have analyzed its problem so clearly and worked out its program so intelligently.

.   .   .

Shortly after the organizing of the United Nations, its management decided its headquarters should be built in Greenwich, Conn., one of the richest and most beautiful suburban communities in the world. The announcement broke with much fanfare.

The citizens of Greenwich, not having been consulted, worried about problems such as water supply, sewage, traffic, housing, property values, and sightseers swarming through the normally quiet back roads.

Two groups formed, one pro and one con. The organization opposed to UN locating in Greenwich employed a public relations counsel who advocated a community opinion study. The tabulations revealed that a majority of the citizenry opposed having UN headquarters in the town but, it was not certain that this majority would stick together and win the vote in a meeting at which the opinion of the citizens would be officially expressed.

The Town of Greenwich covers a fairly big area, some commercial and industrial; some sections have a population with Italian and Portuguese national backgrounds. In some districts the houses are of only moderate value; in others there are fine homes, mansions. Many of the men commute to New York City to work; others have jobs in Greenwich, Stamford, or other nearby towns; some are retired.

Analysis gave a fair blueprint of what people in each part of town and with varying interests knew about the UN question, and the nature of their reasoning and their emotions. On some points the public relations campaign was broadcast to the whole citizenry. In several districts special points were covered in neighborhood meetings.

The research had to be conducted and interpreted within a few days, because of the nearness of the approaching town referendum vote. The research, the analysis, and the campaign built around it turned out successfully, despite the haste. The forces favoring the UN site in Greenwich might have won the referendum. But apparently they did not arm themselves with sufficient knowledge of the feelings and reasoning of the community as a whole and that of the various districts concerned with special problems.

The winning side made it clear all along that it did not oppose

United Nations, but only its locating in Greenwich. One successful device was the confining of its spokesmen strictly to local residents speaking on local problems, and not straying into the subject of the desirability of the world organization.

The community opinion research study early in the campaign not only made possible a correct analysis of public opinion but also gave many residents assurance that their contributions of time and money had an excellent chance of success for the side they favored.

In a battle of minds, as well as in a shooting fight, a commander needs the facts in order to develop sound strategy and action.

Cooperating with Dealers

A pharmaceutical concern, Company M, old in years and youthful in ideas, wanted to know the opinions of pharmacists. It had an alert market research department, which kept itself informed of the trade's inventories and sales of the company's products and those of competitors. But the management had no clear conception of how the pharmacists regarded the company, or "house," in comparison with competing organizations. Also the management was not certain how much influence pharmacists exerted in the selection of branded items specified in prescriptions written by physicians.

In some areas many of the general practitioners in the medical profession own what amounts to a small drugstore in his own back office and frequently doesn't send a patient with a prescription to a pharmacist. But most doctors do not attempt to stock medical supplies, other than for emergencies. The survey in this instance covered the latter group.

Interviewers called on a cross section of pharmacists and asked for opinions regarding which pharmaceutical houses exhibited the most progressiveness in research; which offered the best quality and value of products; which rendered the best service, etc. Then, an alphabetical list of 20 leading houses was presented and each pharmacist was asked to rank several of the companies from various standpoints. The first technique brought out a "free response." The second method, showing a list, double checks—otherwise the interviewee may temporarily forget to mention certain companies which the pharmacist admires.

The result of this survey showed Company M more highly regarded than it thought. This gave the management courage to capitalize more than previously on its existing good will. Also, the company executives became intrigued with the idea of delving more deeply into the subject.

Another technique was then tried out. This consisted of inviting several pharmacists, representing a small cross section in a large city, to a dinner to meet a few of the company's principal officials. After an excellent meal, in a friendly social atmosphere, the officers asked the guests to "take their hair down" and give opinions about a variety of subjects. The opinions came thick and fast, revealing frankness and perception.

The management gave a series of similar dinners in various cities, until a fairly definite pattern took shape. The company was able to draw an up-to-the-minute picture of the minds of people handling its products, how they rated leading drug companies, how they collaborated with physicians in certain respects, and how Company M might improve its position. The two-way flow of knowledge turned out to be highly constructive.

You don't know much about what people think or feel unless you talk with them or get someone else to do so. What you learned a few years ago may be antiquated. It pays to know closely what your publics think and how they feel about things if you would understand a situation and figure out how to improve it.

What the Owners Think

While interviewing usually is the more satisfactory technique in opinion research, a questionnaire mailed to a fairly homogeneous, well-informed group has proved to be valid and productive, especially where there is a high percentage of returns.

Some publicly-owned companies today occasionally enclose a questionnaire with a dividend check to stockholders—the real owners. Many enjoy being asked for their opinions and offer some helpful suggestions.

Mr. Jackson, chairman of the board of a company with 80,000 holders of common stock, planned an issue of a large amount of preferred stock to finance the company's expansion program. He expected reluctance on the part of the common stockholders regarding the dividend priority for the buyers of the preferred issue. He wanted present common stockholders to buy liberally into the new issue, thus strengthening the market value of the company's securities. There had been trouble at the annual stockholder meetings due to persons who challenged various company policies and thereby threatened to cause unfavorable stories in the financial press.

Mr. Jackson authorized a questionnaire addressed to stockholders. He asked for their opinions, not only on the form of the annual and interim reports but also on policies regarding expansion, keeping dividends moderate in order to plow money back into the business, etc. Analysis of the answers gave him an idea of the state of mind of the investors. With this knowledge, he stepped up his stockholder relations program.

Letters from stockholders were answered promptly and thoroughly by a top ranking officer. Stockholders who visited or phoned to company headquarters were treated with courtesy and given frank and complete answers to questions. With each dividend check a small house organ was enclosed to keep recipients well informed on company activities and policies.

Before each annual meeting of stockholders, Mr. Jackson was thoroughly coached regarding any of the scores of questions which might come from the floor. He was prepared to give correct and useful answers. Also he was emotionally armed to handle possible heckling with good nature and dispatch.

This campaign of good stockholder relations was sincere, was continued, and amicable relationships grew. Its success can be attributed to understanding stockholders' opinions and attitudes and then doing something constructive as a result of this understanding.

Consulting the Consumer and Citizen

The principal targets of opinion research are either consumers or the general public.

Company N, in a consumer goods business, each year made a study to learn how housewives and certain opinion molders rated the company in relation to its competitors. Questions were asked about sales and advertising, progressiveness in research, and quality and value of the industry's products.

After learning the attitudes of consumers, the company could shape its policies and practices more intelligently so that they would be understood and liked by the public. Each year the company's rating rose and so did its sales and earnings.

Early in this process, the management found that the public had little knowledge of, or appreciation for, the company's scientific research program. So the public was told about it, in terms of benefits to consumers.

Another early weakness revealed by the opinion studies was

in relationships with teachers and home economists. This resulted in the company searching for what these particular publics needed and desired, and then taking suitable action. Naturally, their good will toward Company N started to climb.

Many consumers, opinion study showed, confused Company N with a competitor which had a somewhat similar name. To offset this and to achieve greater good will, Company N started an institutional advertising campaign which helped to build a distinctive personality for itself.

Company N produced dozens of branded products. One of them was Brand Y. Opinion research had shown several years ago that 25% of the housewives knew Brand Y was manufactured by Company N and seemed to regard the connection between the product and the company favorably. Therefore, through its advertising, the company stressed the fact that Brand Y was a member of the Company N family of products. So each year more and more of the customers knew of the relationship.

•   •   •

A public relations counselor used opinion research to define some problems for a group of food manufacturers. He found, for instance, that the words "food industry" meant one thing to the general public and something different to several of his sponsors.

To the general public, "food industry" didn't include farmers or grocers. Also excluded were meat and milk processors, although a high degree of manufacturing is involved. The public thought that products of the food industry comprised such things as breakfast cereals, crackers, and canned products. The word "industry" apparently brings up in the public's mind a picture of a factory.

In the thinking of some of the sponsors, "food industry" encompassed agriculture, processing of all food products, and their warehousing, wholesaling, and retailing. Without opinion research they might have continued to use a term and a concept which the public did not grasp.

Opinion study points the way to a choice of solutions. Either talk in terms the public already understands, or explain the broader meaning of the industry's scope over and over until the people finally accept the sponsor's idea.

• • •

The best known opinion research consists of polls on political issues and candidates. Forecasts of elections, notably inaccurate on a few occasions, tend to obscure the fact that they almost always range within a few percentage points of exactness.

Opinion researchers in 1948 reported that President Truman would not be elected. This was based largely on interviews up to two or three weeks prior to the election. But analysis of the reports of the pollsters in the last several days before Election Day showed a sudden shift taking place in public opinion. The sharp change in the trend was publicized only slightly. Also, millions of Republicans, convinced by the early reports that their party would win, stayed away from the polls.

After each error, methods used by opinion researchers get a healthful overhauling.

While studies about candidates attract the most attention, knowledge of the status of public opinion on *issues* renders the greatest service.

For instance, a study reported that only a minority of the public knew about the work of the commission headed by former President Herbert Hoover to point the way to more efficiency and economy in government. It disappointed many public-spirited citizens to find so few voters well-informed on this subject. But the discovery incited supporters of the activity to promote it to the public more vigorously.

The American public seems to have more progressiveness and vision than many politicians. This has been made clear time after time by comparing nationwide opinion polls with the actions of Congress and the executive branch of the Government at Washington. For instance, the public has consistently marched ahead of the Government in attitudes about national defense and about efficient and economical handling of public affairs.

However, opinion polls clarifying public support for an issue—adequate air power, for instance—give courage and support to legislators, who are bedeviled by local and minority interests of all kinds. Published opinion studies supply them with a ladder to objectivity.

Other Desirable Opinion Studies

Often a rather limited problem can be put on the road to solution through an opinion study.

Mr. Kavanagh admired his company's scientific research achievements. For reasons that he didn't fathom, the science editors and writers paid little attention to his company's scientific news releases.

After opinion research, he found out the heart of the problem and signposts for solving it. Mr. Kavanagh's scientific personnel had been too conservative in its handling of the press. Insufficient information had been issued. Releases came too late to be newsworthy. Also, the science writers were somewhat unfamiliar with Mr. Kavanagh's company, personnel, and activities.

A policy of providing more liberal data was put into effect. Writers received important news far enough in advance to digest it properly. Every consideration was given to timing to fit the news deadlines of the writers, as far as practicable. Writers were invited to visit the laboratory and meet the company's officials. Those who could not be contacted personally were kept informed by mail. After a few years of this kind of work, Mr. Kavanagh felt that he was receiving all the cooperation he could reasonably expect.

Mr. London, an ethical drug manufacturer, wanted opinions of several dozen deans of accredited medical schools. He couldn't spare the time to call on them personally, so he mailed them a letter and questionnaire. Most of the deans replied at considerable length, giving valuable ideas and guidance.

The reasons for the fine results included:

1. The subject keenly interested both Mr. London and the deans. For example, questions covered such subjects as grants and fellowships for the schools.
2. In addition to rather down-to-earth items, the survey had the appeal of broader significance—the best possible relationships between education and industry and the welfare of the medical profession, especially regarding future physicians.

Opinion surveys have been made in countless special groups, such as teachers of penmanship, industrialists, labor union leaders, lawyers, gardeners, contributors to a charity, and so on and on.

When well planned and followed through such studies have contributed to locating basic problems and formulating solutions.

Sidelights on Making a Survey

We merely touch upon the techniques of making an opinion survey. There is excellent literature on the subject, and there are many specialists available. The best way to conduct a study is to work with one of these specialists. An amateur job may result both in wrong answers and confusion or resentment.

However, here are a few observations to keep in mind:

1. Get professional advice.
2. Use one or more pilot studies, whenever practicable, to make the wording understandable in order to bring forth useful answers. In case of a mail survey, experiment until you get a high rate of return which will be fairly representative. In one instance, a pilot study of 100 mailed questionnaires brought back only 10 replies. The second, improved pilot study resulted in 25 out of the 100. The third pilot, still further developed, produced almost a 50 per cent return.
3. Be sure the subject matter interests your audience.
4. Include, whenever practicable, two major appeals—one to the material instincts of the respondent and one to his nobler interests. For instance, a minister naturally wants a large, generous membership in his church. Also he hopes to advance the cause of religion generally. A housewife likes to talk about her own interests and at the same time to give information of value to other homemakers.
5. Be sure you interpret the findings correctly. Many times someone will pick out a few intriguing details of a survey and miss the real nuggets.
6. Watch for undertones—or overtones. Few surveys can dredge up everything you would like to know about opinions and emotions of a public you deal with.
7. Keep up to date. A study you made a few years ago may be obsolete today. Don't base your reasoning on old attitudes, which may have changed radically.
8. So, make prompt use of findings while fresh and authentic.
9. Although personal interviews—especially long, thorough ones—usually give the clearest information, sometimes a

mail survey will produce equally good or even better results. This applies in case of a homogeneous, well-informed group, and when a sufficiently large percentage replies. This has been proved by use of interviews followed by a double check with mailed questionnaires. A man in one of the professions, with a crowded waiting room, may give brusque comments to an interviewer. But later on, alone in his library, he may write out thoughtful answers to printed questions. A respondent sometimes will unburden his mind and soul on a sheet of paper whereas he might not do so for a stranger looking at him across a cluttered desk.

10. Leave to a specialist the complex techniques of planning, the selection of a cross section of your public, the framing of questions, and the tabulations. But cooperate with him in every possible way by supplying him with useful information.

Some public relations practitioners overemphasize the role of opinion research. They may try to substitute it for keen perception and sound judgment. Other public relations consultants and corporation executives pooh-pooh opinion research and rely on their intuition—sometimes effectively and sometimes not. In between these extremes lies the sound course.

In Review

To summarize this chapter, opinion research offers a powerful tool for isolating basic problems and laying the groundwork for strategy in solving them. No matter how brilliant the day-to-day tactics, they are less important than a sound underlying strategy built on knowledge and understanding.

No employer can really understand the opinions and attitudes of hundreds or thousands of employes without use of some scientific opinion research. He should follow up his findings with prompt action. This brings about improved human relationships.

To understand a community's attitudes, one doesn't study the rooftops. He goes to the front doors and talks things over with the people. He learns what the community generally thinks—also attitudes of residents in different districts and with special interests.

An organization which sells through dealers usually accepts the fact that they are vital to its business. So, it pays to know their opinions and to take needed action to offset ill will and to build good will.

Stockholders own a business, and it pays to learn their attitudes. Stockholders are human beings first and investors second. They appreciate getting cordial treatment, having their opinions asked, and receiving adequate information. In many instances, stockholders can influence a company's sales, and its reputation with the public.

The general public, both as consumers and as citizens, may swing over to a point of view you wish to establish. But first you must understand them. To do so, there is no real substitute for opinion research.

Words sometimes engrave an image in the general public's mind different from the way a management sees it. Therefore, opinion research may be advisable on key words or phrases to get your meaning grasped correctly by the public.

While opinion polls on political candidates have sometimes missed the mark badly, they usually come close to being accurate. Polls of the public regarding political issues are presumably accurate and they aid opinion leaders, including legislators.

This chapter does not attempt to go thoroughly into the subject of opinion research per se, but rather into some of its applications to public relations. From that standpoint, ten general comments are made: 1) Get professional advice; 2) use pilot studies whenever practicable; 3) interest your audience; 4) if you can, appeal to both the material and the nobler interests of people; 5) interpret findings with keen judgment; 6) watch for undertones; 7) keep surveys up to date; 8) make use of findings promptly before they get stale; 9) while interviews usually are preferable, mail surveys fill the bill in some instances; 10) cooperate with a research specialist by giving him useful information, but leave techniques up to him.

Opinion research is a powerful aid—not a substitute—for keen perception and sound judgment.

CHAPTER IX ⟩ **Discarding Non-Essentials**

Sometimes a young person shows signs of ability to pursue successfully any one of several careers. He might become a portrait painter, a pianist, an author, a baseball professional, or business executive. He cannot possibly excel in all. He would be wise to eliminate the careers of least interest to him and those in which he thinks he will be least proficient. He gradually narrows his course down to one or possibly two, and concentrates his study and effort. Of course, he retains a lesser interest or two for a hobby or avocation.

To an extent, this situation repeats itself in pinning down the core of a public relations problem. You use a process of elimination.

· · · ·

Leaders in an industry association worried about several human relations problems. They listed 15 ideas they thought should be explained to the public. Actually, it is not easy to get the public to grasp firmly just one basic idea about an industry or an organization. Even in high level controversy, it is hard to get public opinion aware of more than three of the issues at stake.

It was because the industry leaders were so close to their work that all 15 items seemed vital. For instance, one point had to do with an incident that occurred 20 years ago. It still rankled in the minds of the industrialists, but the public wouldn't be interested.

Another item had to do with a legal problem, difficult to explain and of no real interest to anyone except the insiders. So, one after another those things which would have no appeal to the general public dropped by the wayside. The points selected to sell to the public boiled down to three. One proved so vital and interesting that all major efforts concentrated around it. Thus the industry won the recognition and good will it sought. With its efforts scattered in 15 directions and thus weakened, the entire project would have failed.

Omit the Unsupported Assumption

One of the first things to eliminate from a hodgepodge of subjects is any factor with an element of doubtful truth—or something based on an unsupported assumption.

Let's look in at the board room of Company O. The executive committee is in session. For weeks the management representatives have negotiated with a labor union group about a new contract. Both sides have kept rather reasonable but their nerves now are frazzled. The union members have authorized their officers to call a strike if the contract cannot be agreed upon. A strike, if called, would presumably last for several weeks and would cost the company and employes and their families millions of dollars.

Only one fairly minor point remains unsettled. Both sides feel they have made all concessions within reason. Their "backs are up." A public relations consultant sits in with the management's executive committee, because a strike would have definite bearing on the company's relations with the public. He hears that the chief reason the management refuses to make any further concession is that the officers "want to back up the company's supervisors."

Union officers and stewards have taken over some of the influence and prestige that normally belongs to foremen and superintendents in the plants. The management wants to restore the proper authority and self-respect of these supervisors. The works manager states that it is time for a show-down if the foremen under his direction can ever "hold their heads up again."

The consultant asks and gets permission to interview a cross section of the foremen. The foremen hear the story of the negotiations, the nature of the final stumbling block, and the consequences of a long, costly strike. Then the foremen are asked, in view of the facts, whether the concession to the union would or would not be justified and whether it would be a reflection on their own status.

Nearly every one of them decides that the concession "makes sense" in this instance and that it would hurt neither his prestige nor his feelings. In this way, by eliminating a bogey, the management sees the real problem clearly and is able to go about settling it.

When Emotions Upset Reason

In clearing away the underbrush surrounding a complex problem, look for places where emotions have eclipsed reason. To do this you should be able to truss up your own emotions temporarily in order to understand those of other people and to see things with clear, calm eyes.

Mr. Malden presided over the executive committee of a company which relied heavily upon advertising. Studies showed that the current advertising campaign had become blunted in effectiveness. A new fillip seemed urgent. The advertising director and agency found a happy way out. They acquired a short term option on one of the best of the humorous radio programs, a "natural" for the company.

Mr. Malden didn't happen to like radio in any form except for newscasts and classical music. He expounded on this point to his advertising personnel. Mr. Malden was told that he would be invited to go to the auditions—in the hope of winning his interest. But this merely sounded like extra and annoying work to him.

Then the chairman of the board stepped in. He pointed out to Mr. Malden that it would be helpful if he could forget for the moment his personal likes and dislikes and get to the gist of the problem. He jokingly remarked, "I guess the boys tried to do a little selling when they suggested that you go to some of the auditions. You and I would be nuisances if we did attend."

Mr. Malden, ordinarily objective, saw the point and discarded his emotional road block. He then listened to a review of the facts and accepted the idea for the new advertising campaign.

A different radio problem confronted Mr. Newcomb. Among many other duties, he supervised two network programs for his company, on excellent evening hours with a high degree of listenership.

Mr. Newcomb liked popular music and entertainment and enjoyed listening to almost any good program. In fact, he liked radio so much he felt impelled to handle many of the details ordinarily assigned to specialists, chiefly in the advertising agencies. Yet, these details annoyed him almost to distraction. Furthermore, he would not authorize sufficient funds for the highest grade of talent, and finally recommended to the management that it abandon the network shows entirely.

The management, somewhat disturbed about giving up franchises on choice radio time, looked into the problem. One officer spoke up: "Mr. Newcomb likes radio, but he likes it so much he won't let go of the complex, specialized operation which the advertising agency should take care of, with any needed cooperation from our advertising department. I recommend that we keep our program running for another year, with Mr. Newcomb contributing only on basic policy questions. During the coming year let's explore the advisability of spending money to produce top ranking shows with top sales results."

These suggestions were adopted, and Mr. Newcomb now had time to handle his various tasks. By the end of the 12-months period, the network shows improved and so did the company's sales. By clearing away emotional factors, the management had looked at the problem squarely and then solved it.

Many times a problem is not properly understood in advertising and other functions. One powerful and ingenious trade association secretary was assigned a budget to promote good will for an industry. He arranged to have too much of the promotion center on extolling himself and the association rather than the industry and its products and services.

One advertising campaign put its emphasis on the customers of the company's products. The "you" approach appeared throughout, with every indication of successful results. But the committee in charge decided to switch to a "we" approach. One member wanted to have much of the advertising praise the company's factories and machinery. Others sought promotion about the company's purchasing power; laboratories; dealers, and export business. The result was a potpourri, with expensive art work and competent copy, to be sure, but with the spark of good public relations and advertising gone.

An Eye to the Future

In analyzing a problem, be sure to study whether too much weight is put on the past and too little on the present and future. Deep down, the instincts and emotions of human nature change slowly. But the public's mind always changes—probably mostly for the better.

Miss Oliver, a practitioner with a long, successful record, feels that she has experienced just about everything in public relations work. Techniques she has been using for 10 or 15 years seem to be effective. She thinks, "So, why shouldn't they continue to work?" They might and then again they might not, because of changing conditions. Public relations must be geared both to people fundamentally and also to their shifting habits, environments, and viewpoints.

She embarks upon a new assignment with Company P. On the surface, the problem looks nearly identical to one with which she had struggled a decade ago. She applies most of her old techniques and fortunately they work fairly well. Then she runs out of her supply of former experiences and tells her superior that the job is completed.

Her chief happens to live primarily in the present and future. Within an hour, he outlines a dozen new steps which should be taken or at least considered, in view of the special problem of Company P and the conditions it faces or probably will encounter.

Experiences of the past have tremendous value, but their significance always should be weighed in the light of a rapidly moving world, and the public's craving for new and better ideas and things.

Another woman learned the value of change of pace in public relations. She did a brilliant public relations job in the food field. She created new and stimulating ideas. Then her assignment changed to work for a cosmetic industry. She leaned heavily on her previous experience but soon found her methods in-apropos to her new work.

At first she failed to realize that she faced an almost entirely different problem, calling for different treatment. After learning some of the fundamental and unique facts about the cosmetic business, she proceeded to strike out with novel and appropriate ideas. She could adapt some of her former training, but relied chiefly on creation of projects which, so far as she knew, had never been attempted before in quite the same form.

Cutting a Gordian Knot

When you unravel a knotty problem and find its focal point, try to make it understood by those around you. Keep pounding away at explaining your discovery with patient persistence.

In a fairly large city, serving a 50-mile radius, which needed new hospitals, civic leaders drew up a proposal for merging existing hospitals and their boards of governors. The consolidation was to be followed by a fund-raising campaign for new buildings, with contributions in sight both from the citizens and governmental sources.

Some of the existing hospitals were well-managed and financially solvent, others not. The boards of governors consisted chiefly of merchants, manufacturers, bankers, lawyers, and wealthy retired persons. Physicians did not serve on these boards but in medical staff groups instead.

A series of misunderstandings and disagreements broke out between the physicians and the board members over a long period. Tension and acrimony increased and it became exceedingly difficult to unravel dozens of knotted strands.

After considerable study, a consultant decided to try cutting the Gordian knot. He believed that the center of the problem was to get the two warring elements together, through an intermediary, so that any one of several reasonable solutions could be weighed. Although the consultant was engaged by one side in the controversy, he accepted the appointment with the feeling that his efforts would be on behalf of the public which needed and wanted improved hospital facilities. Settling the controversy would serve as a means of rendering a real service to the public.

He agreed to do all he could to inform the public of the facts in the controversy, not to save face for anyone but in the hope of laying groundwork for eventual understanding and cooperation in a community project to be developed with fairness and efficiency. He concentrated upon the heart of the problem—how to get the opponents together on some sensible basis. Time after time both sides would agree to make moves toward that end. But then someone would say or do something which would cause tempers to erupt again.

The solution finally arrived at is too complicated to explain in this short illustration. The point to be remembered, however, is the effort to offset hurt feelings, misunderstandings, errors in judgment and diplomacy, and many other factors, in the single-track drive toward gaining an honorable peace in the public's interest.

A Secret of General Management

Another example of finding the keystone of a complicated group of problems appears in Company Q, whose board chairman was Mr. Peel. This company, in the grocery products business, is regarded as one of the nation's best-managed organizations. Mr. Peel was asked what his major problem was and how he isolated it.

"When I first stepped into my present job," said Mr. Peel, "I was frankly confused by what at times seemed to be a bedlam of contradictory interests and viewpoints.

"We received letters from stockholders requesting that we increase our dividends. Some of the largest stockholders called on me personally to ask for a boost in dividend rates. If we had increased the rate on the basis of earnings at that time, we would have had to abandon plowing part of the profits into needed expansion. Also, we couldn't have given moderate wage rises which seemed warranted.

"Our labor union demanded much higher wage scales," Mr. Peel said. "To agree would mean cutting down on one or more other activities, such as advertising and research, upon which we relied to go ahead in our race with competition.

"The Purchasing Department sought to build up larger inventories, but that would have strained our cash position. The Sales Department desired numerous price reductions. Our scientists wished to expand their personnel and facilities.

"Demands from nearly every direction—most of them in head-on conflict with one another. So, I finally realized that my major problem was *to strike the fairest possible balance among these warring stresses and strains and come forth with the best coordination I could conceive.*

"I had to know enough about each department to understand its contributions and its needs. But I determined not to try to *run* any department. That must be delegated to the responsible executives.

"I saw that I must help adjust their differences, get them to understand the limitations of the organization as a whole, and work together as a team. I also had to be a salesman to get certain executives to see the overall blueprint of the complex, sensitively balanced mechanism of the company.

"Of course, many kinds of problems, big and little, arise in running a business. But the most continuous major problem is coordination—finding the best balance. A general manager should be something like an orchestra leader, getting each musician to contribute just the right quality and quantity to get the best general effect for the audience."

Mr. Peel's perception of this main problem of general management advanced him well along the road to its solution.

In a book entitled *Sharing a Business,* by Franklin J. Lunding, chief executive officer of Jewel Tea Co., Inc., published by the Updegraff Press, Ltd., one of many excellent statements follows:

"A primary obligation of management today is to think, plan and work with an increased sense of social responsibility, to try earnestly to share equitably the productivity of enterprise in terms of goods and services, salaries and wages, satisfactions of the mind and spirit, leisure and security. If one group—any group—demands an unfair share of what a business produces, it is the duty of management to say 'No.'

"In this sense, whether he realizes it or not, the business manager is a technician in sharing. Whatever else he does, if he is to manage successfully he must master the art of balancing the rights and interests of the various groups which play a part in the success of the business."

In Review

In this chapter we have suggested a few ideas showing how to discard non-essentials and get down to fundamentals of a public relations problem.

One method is the process of elimination. Some managements wish to convey a mass of information which is too extensive and complex to be grasped by the public. And much of it would not be of interest to many persons except those in management. You do well if you can firmly establish a single thought about your project in the public's mind.

Eliminate any idea of questionable truth or any unsupported assumption. You must have facts to back you up.

Try to lock out thinking which gets twisted by wrought up emotions or by too much subjectivity. For instance, an association secretary put too much emphasis on building his own prestige and that of his organization rather than the industry and its products and services.

Before repeating techniques successful in the past, review them carefully to be reasonably sure they will be effective today and tomorrow in the light of rapidly changing conditions. Always be ready for a change of pace and be open-minded about new ideas.

In a badly snarled situation you may have to cut the Gordian knot and start afresh with single-minded purpose, with an idea which makes sense. This applied to a complicated controversy in a community which wanted a medical center. Another example was the chief executive officer who found that his real problem was not trying to run every activity of his organization, but to co-ordinate conflicting interests as fairly and as wisely as possible.

CHAPTER X } **Developing Strategy**

AFTER CLARIFYING a public relations problem you may have a choice of several ways of trying to solve it. These will depend somewhat upon the nature of the problem. But a general formula applies in many instances.

Rogers, Slade & Hill, a firm of management consultants, in its publication, *Management Briefs,* offers one interesting approach. It applies to almost any problem arising in business—not to public relations alone. *Public Relations Journal,* December, 1951, reprinted this formula under the heading, "Nine Rules for Solving Problems," as follows:

> "Here are nine rules for meeting business problems, written by a man who seems never to be stumped by any problem that comes up in his business:
>
> "1. Crystallize the problem so that it can be clearly expressed in a simple statement or question.
>
> "2. Get all the pertinent facts and figures.
>
> "3. Organize them objectively, not to make a case or prove a point, but to get at the reality of the problem.
>
> "4. Call together those who might contribute to the solution to the problem.
>
> "5. Explain the problem and present the facts to this group, simply, fully, and without color or bias, and without suggesting your own solution if you think you have one.
>
> "6. Ask for suggestions, calling on each person to outline his ideas briefly, withholding your arguments or objections.
>
> "7. Throw the subject open for general discussion, keeping it to the point but letting it run as long as anyone has anything of value to contribute.

"8. Arrive at a decision if possible; if not, consign the problem for further study and set a definite time for another meeting.

"9. Meanwhile, don't fret or worry, for worry aggravates problems and makes them increasingly difficult to solve."

•   •   •

All the elements in the management firm's formula seem practical in dealing with a problem. In this book, however, we want to extend them and tailor them to public relations.

One of the first steps in solving a public relations problem is to shape a basic strategy. Several illustrations will be given in this chapter. Some show an unavoidable overlap with other subjects, such as techniques to be used in a subsequent program. But all the examples pinpoint some type or phase of strategy.

If your study has shown the presence of abuses which cause ill will, these should be cleared up, if possible, and replaced with action and interpretation which create understanding and good will.

For instance, there were abuses in used car advertising and sales methods in a large city. The local newspapers, cooperating with the Better Business Bureau and elements of business and industry, largely eliminated the abuses by sustained, intelligent effort to educate the public and by policing the advertising.

A factory with poor washroom facilities, inferior lighting and ventilation, careless housekeeping, and numerous little hazards to safety was cleaned up. This resulted in noticeable improvements in personnel attitudes and in productivity.

A plant which deposited fly ash on the washings on clotheslines in the neighborhood converted effectively to a different type of fuel and better equipment, thus improving the community's attitude toward the plant.

A large distributor who had tried to overload his dealers with merchandise revamped his policy to one of supplying only the dealers' approximate needs and helping to promote their sales more vigorously.

A large industry advertised its product in a manner which the public considered to be tricky and in questionable taste. These facts were recognized by the sponsor, and the advertising changed to a new approach based on good taste.

You can find countless instances of the clearing up of abuses as an opening gun in the strategy for handling a public relations problem. At times, the ending of an abuse or nuisance is so obvious that it is unnecessary or even unwise to talk about it. But in most cases you should inform all who might be interested. Otherwise they might not know of the improvement for a long time.

Occasionally a business organization faces a stone wall, at least temporarily, in regard to correcting what the public regards as an abuse. The producer of a household gadget normally made entirely of metal, cannot get enough of the metal. He uses substitute materials which do not satisfy the housewife customer. A medium-sized company, having a hard time keeping out of the red, cannot afford some major improvements which employes and the community think should be made in the factory. Another company can afford such changes but can't get the equipment. If an abuse cannot be liquidated, this fact should be explained frankly and clearly to everyone concerned.

Diversion from Bad to Good Symbols

After planning to correct abuses or explaining any cul de sac, the next logical step in strategy is to divert attention to things that will build good will.

When things go badly for the party in power at Washington, the public's attention is constantly shifted to some action or statement which seems constructive.

On the heels of a major airline crash, railroad wreck, or some other calamity, the powers-that-be order investigations immediately. To some extent this shifts the focus to a collateral activity, gives promise of punishment if called for, and implies corrective action for the future.

The diversion of public attention from bad to good symbols should be thought of in terms of the long-range future and not merely "to get out of a hole." Good public relations look years ahead. Even if you embark on a short-term project, such as the celebration of a department store's 100th anniversary, you should plan to combine timely interest with lasting good will.

The O.P.A. Case

Let's examine several major examples of strategy formation. It is undesirable in some cases to use the names of the industries and individuals involved. To do so, we, in all fairness, would have to go into much greater detail, discuss all angles, and get numerous O.K.'s. We have boiled a few illustrations down to bring out how strategy has been successfully developed.

Mention of the name of the one-time Office of Price Administration is needed, however, to tell the following story:

In the early days of 1946, the work of O.P.A. was generally popular with a large majority of the public. Many goods were scarce, and fears of inflation widespread.

Anticipating a rapid return to ample supplies of merchandise, several businessmen developed a strategy for bringing about an early demise for O.P.A. Numerous abuses had arisen in the administration of price controls. Black markets flourished and threatened to become a national scandal. In the case of meat, unsanitary handling by black marketeers endangered public health. Operations of competitive enterprise were disrupted. Useful companies faced financial failure. Employes were being laid off in some communities.

No single group of business people handled the overall campaign to end O.P.A. There were several groups and many individuals. But they did tend to gravitate generally around the strategy developed by a few of the leading thinkers.

At first the efforts failed badly. Angry speeches, interviews, and news releases were issued. These had little effect on the general public. It should be remembered that the public pays little heed to anyone who sounds angry or otherwise overly aroused emotionally. "He's off his rocker," Mr. Public thinks, shrugging his shoulders. Also, the spokesmen were usually heads of large business associations or companies. The public felt these men had selfish interests and were not sufficiently concerned with the "little fellow."

Another technique was tried briefly in the form of temperate, watered-down promotion, but it sounded too scholarly—almost as though it had been written by economists for an academic publication. Opinion research showed that this approach made little impression on the public.

Then, effective strategy began to take shape. Public relations workers knew that when a large portion of the public is in favor of something, such as O.P.A., there must be an intermediate step in shifting the attitude. First, the public mind must be won over to the idea of recognizing reasonable doubt and having an open mind.

This was accomplished in a variety of ways. In nearly every locality the evils of the growing local black markets were exposed, with the idea of getting the public to take a second look at the problem with fairness and objectivity. Facts were brought out, not in terms of theory but of a roast of beef and a pound of butter, to show how O.P.A. was creating scarcity instead of plenty and holding many prices up higher than needed. Congressmen and their constituents were told in detail of havoc created at the local level. The approach to the public was concentrated in terms of the average citizen, family, and community and things people need to eat, to wear, and to enjoy reasonable comforts.

Many individual restrictions seemed ridiculous when scrutinized, and these rapidly melted away under fire from Congressmen, the press, and other forces.

Before long, Mr. and Mrs. Public decided they should take a second look at the problem—that there were two sides to the question. (Of course, many people became merely confused.) But in this frame of mind they listened attentively to the continuing and mounting campaign which made frontal attacks demanding the abolition of price controls generally.

Before the end of 1946, public opinion had made an almost complete swing of the pendulum. Only a small minority now favored the price control set-up. This unusually sudden shift was not entirely due to strategy and educational efforts. Various events and trends speeded things up. But the emergence of effective strategy was unquestionably a strong factor.

A Right-about-Face in Strategy

Mr. Quincy, a figure in public life, got his name on front pages of newspapers frequently by attacking an industry familiar to almost every home. The industry leaders angrily denounced him at every opportunity. They not only attacked his statements, but also the man personally.

Mr. Quincy, having a kind of tantrum complex, wanted attention for himself even though unfavorable. He kept piling up stronger abuse, resulting in more heated replies. The public became increasingly annoyed both with Mr. Quincy and with the industry.

Accepting public relations advice, the industry leaders decided to ignore completely the attacks of their critic. The consultant explained to them that pursuing their present course only made matters worse and that a change in strategy seemed definitely in order. Of course, there are situations in which leaving a critic unanswered would be a mistake. In this instance, the feud had reached almost the limit of vituperation and conditions had deteriorated so badly that only a drastic change—a fresh start— would be effective.

The industry leaders concentrated on taking constructive action which deserved the public's good will and made sure the public understood it. They even praised their erstwhile critic whenever he did or said something which warranted praise.

Mr. Quincy, hungry for publicity, did not receive so much of it as formerly, but what he did get was mostly favorable. He liked his new role better than his former one and played along with it. He did some things helpful for those he formerly had attacked bitterly.

The general public had little awareness of what had gone on behind the scenes but at least felt relieved of the annoyance of the constant feuding. This is one example of enlightened public relations strategy working out well for both the principal actors in the drama and the public—the audience.

The Trial Balloon

Company R, owned by many thousands of stockholders, including high-grade, conservative institutions, such as charities, colleges, orphanages, and religious institutions, had built a fine name for its integrity and public spirit.

Along came an opportunity to acquire a controlling interest in another company in an industry looked upon with disfavor by many persons. The acquisition promised a handsome profit for

Company R, but the management worried about repercussions with some of its employes, dealers, customers, stockholders, and public opinion generally.

The strategy used in meeting this problem may seem short-range on the surface, but actually it looked to the future.

Company R issued a statement to the press that a month later its board of directors would vote on the question of its entry into the new industry. This was a so-called "trial balloon," frequently used in politics. The statement to the press was widely reported. Shouts of protest broke out from nearly all of Company R's publics. The idea of the acquisition was promptly dropped. The company proceeded to maintain and build good will. The test it had made may be considered only a technique—actually it was part and parcel of enduring strategy, of looking carefully before leaping.

Members of a Team

One large industry, for years a political whipping boy, so far as the public realized, consisted chiefly of five or six huge companies. The products of this industry interested practically every family in the United States. But the managers and directors of the few leading companies had only a handful of votes in political elections. The customers were so numerous they could elect or defeat a candidate, or decide the outcome of a political issue affecting the industry.

The problem was to present a true picture to the public—and to destroy the myth of only a few super-corporation managements instead of a complex of millions of men, women, and children.

Actually among the thousands of manufacturers in this industry, the few which had grown large had done so mostly through efficiency and quality and value of products and services. They reaped relatively few of the benefits and carried the burden of many of the industry's responsibilities which the smaller members could not assume.

So, a major part of the strategy adopted was to make it clear to the public that the industry was a *team*—a team of millions of producers of raw materials; shippers, distributors, merchants, and processors and their employes. Also, many more millions of customers played in the "game." A correct image of the industry was drawn—not of a few executives but of a far-flung multitude of people working together with a common interest.

Prices of the industry's products seemed to the public unduly high, resulting in widespread complaints. But when the facts were revealed, a long involved chain of operations came into view with each link receiving only a moderate return for its labor.

The symbol of a team is a good one in American Life. When the facts back of such a symbol stand up, as in the case of this industry, the result proves highly constructive.

In Review

You can rely upon a variety of formulae for solving a difficult problem, particularly on the business front. More specifically in a formula for public relations, after you isolate your problem or problems, the forming of strategy becomes a first item on the agenda.

If abuses or nuisances create ill will, these should be corrected or allayed if possible. Otherwise offer suitable explanations.

As another early step, divert attention to ideas, statements, and activities which will tend to build good will, and erase troubles of the past.

The public discounts statements of persons who act highly excited—the public considers their reasoning distorted. Also the public tends to believe those spokesmen credited not with feathering their own nests but with showing a real concern for public welfare.

In shifting public opinion from one viewpoint to an opposite one, there often must be an intermediate phase, during which the public accepts the thought that there are two potent sides to the question at stake. In this state of mind, the people will give both sides of the argument a fairly even break, and the better debater then has a good chance of carrying the day.

It does not pay, in battles of the mind or any other kind, to underestimate your adversary. Don't belittle and insult. Do a good job and explain it well. Sometimes a word of deserved praise for an opponent benefits your own cause and paves the way for eventual harmony and cooperation.

Understanding of your publics' attitudes and utilizing this knowledge in your program, in what may seem temporary situations, can be part of long-range strategy. This does not mean you should blindly follow all whims of your publics—some of them are wrong and can be changed. But if you often range too far afield from your publics' convictions, you can get into serious trouble.

Many good symbols influence American public opinion, for instance, the concept of team play—sharing of effort and responsibility in a common cause. If you have a situation in which such an idea applies and you can prove your case, then make it a steppingstone in your strategy.

CHAPTER XI ⟩ Finding the Theme

AFTER DECIDING upon your basic strategy, look around for a theme. The public isn't likely to recognize an organization's strategy, but it should become conscious of a theme which spearheads that strategy.

A theme may take either the form of a slogan or an idea spelled out over and over in advertising, in editorial material, and in conversation. It must be backed up by performance. Otherwise it eventually may do more harm than good. Sometimes the theme has no definite combination of words but is a composite of impressions which in a united manner penetrate the public's mind and emotions.

For instance, one large department store established the theme that it stocks good merchandise, carefully inspected to assure quality, and sells it at an exceptionally low price, because of its large volume and because it does a cash business.

One motor vehicle company may adopt the theme of having the most efficient service stations. One may stress the craftsmanship of its workers. One speaks frequently of the many combinations of fathers and sons among its employes, indicating pride in the quality of their work and in the company's reputation. Another relies largely on the snob appeal, which after all has quite a niche in human nature.

Colleges and charities, as well as businesses, sometimes develop what amounts to a theme—perhaps not in so many words but in the concentration of impressions on their publics.

Shortly after World War II, the American Association of

Nurserymen, representing nurserymen who sell trees, shrubs, and other plant materials, decided to embark on a public relations project. Their problems were analyzed through interviews with a cross section of members, study of records, and public opinion research.

One of the principal problems was clear at the outset—how to keep a flow of business based on growing public interest and appreciation of the industry's products and services.

In raising his thousands of plants, a nurseryman has a sizable investment extending over a number of years. If the market isn't there when his crops mature, his business is jeopardized.

Research showed that the principal interest of buyers of nursery products was in beauty and enjoyment of trees, shrubs, vines, and other nursery products and services. A second choice was in the economic zone—if a home-owner wanted to sell or rent his house, it would bring a better price if the house were attractively landscaped. Still another economic advantage of planned planting appeared in that proper placement of hedges for windbreaks, shade trees for shade, etc., made the home more livable in both winter and summer by controlling cold winds and shading out the hot sun.

Many other factors came into view—for example, many long-established plantings around homes, factories, or public buildings need reconditioning and replacement. Several types of businesses were represented among the association's members. While most were primarily growers and made sales in a limited area, some sold nursery products nationally from door to door or through mail order or stores.

There were several seasonal latitudes. Many of the plant materials in Florida and California differed radically from those of the northern and central latitudes of the United States.

One major appeal seemed to tie things together—the almost

universal appeal of beauty and enjoyment of good planting. Around that idea much of the strategy centered. The theme evolved into "Plant America."

•   •   •

By leafing through the pages of a magazine, you can read slogans which spell out the themes of many organizations. The themes give a hint of corporate personalities. Many of the phrases extol a product or service. Others emphasize the objectives of institutions. It is on this latter phase that we largely concentrate in this chapter.

One life insurance company devotes practically all its promotion to the idea of improving health and lengthening lives. It has a selfish interest, to be sure, but the public infers that the company deserves good will for its campaign for people's well-being. The "you" approach dominates. The company writes of the reader's welfare—not of its own.

Another life insurance company, with the name of a Revolutionary patriot in its title, builds good will through its theme of sound Americanism, which it carries out superbly in its promotion. Still another stresses the idea of security—both for the individual and the policy he may hold in this company.

To elaborate on an earlier illustration in this book, one organization which sells products for cleanliness in the home and for personal good grooming crystallizes its theme around developing and otherwise helping people. This beams specifically at the housewife and, through her, at the family. The company provides quality wares at moderate prices and teaches the customers how to save time and backaches with its products. It has aided thousands of persons, handicapped physically or economically, in gaining independence through work in the distribution of company products.

A similar idea carries through among its employes. Over a period of years, workers in the company can attain independence financially. Also the worker gets every reasonable chance for happiness in his work, recreation, health, and security. Even the company's charitable contributions center upon developing human beings.

The principal emphasis is where it should be, namely, that the company is not giving a "handout" but is aiding people to help themselves.

A flour milling company has a theme, not expressed in so many words, of showing interest in others—in being friendly. Of course, this and numerous other themes are offshoots of the Golden Rule. And why not?

One name which should be mentioned here is Du Pont. For generations it manufactured explosives, and in this field contributed importantly to winning World War I. Even before this conflict, however, it had begun a program of diversification that took it into a number of chemical areas. In the decade following World War I, it entered among others the dyestuffs field, as well as the manufacture of rayon and cellophane. And in 1927 it began a program of fundamental research that was to produce nylon and synthetic rubber, along with many other important developments.

Thus when Du Pont was attacked as a "merchant of death" in the Nye Committee hearings of the middle thirties—and this at a time when its production of military explosives was less than 2 per cent of its total production—a highly inaccurate picture was presented. It was as part of a long-range program to correct this popular misunderstanding that the "Better Things for Better Living . . . through Chemistry" theme was devised. The theme is based on fact, and has become recognized by the public.

In Review

Every successful enterprise has within itself the makings of an idea or expression which explains its ideals or its main service to the public. As part of the solution of a problem over an extensive period, a theme assists your publics to understand and appreciate your project.

The theme selected should be truthful. Preferably it should have the "you" angle, not emphasizing the organization so much as the beneficiaries of its work. It should be repeated constantly in order to be recognized. It should be supported by action and evidence of such action. The best themes hinge in some way directly or indirectly on the Golden Rule.

A single organization might try to establish several themes, appealing to varied publics. But preferably concentrate upon the one with the greatest significance to all publics simultaneously. In any event, try to find and use a suitable theme in carrying out your solution of a public relations problem.

CHAPTER XII } **Devices to Dramatize the Theme**

Aᴼᴛᴇʀ ʟɪɴɪɴɢ ᴜᴘ your strategy and theme for the solution of a major problem, you bring into play devices to dramatize your story to the public. To carry out your project you must utilize the senses of the public—what it can see or hear, and occasionally what it can smell.

Mr. and Mrs. Public can see an office and factory. Callers at an office notice keenly how reception rooms and individual offices look. A minor revolution has taken place in the furnishing and decoration of offices. More and more of them exhibit the decor of a living room or library, implying comfort and gracious living. Much progress has been made in lighting, air conditioning, and design of furniture and equipment.

Many factories still harbor junk piles and weeds. But public relations nudges factories into dressing up with attractive landscaping when practicable. A public-eyesore kind of factory symbolizes poor public relations.

Management is also increasingly awakening to the importance of the inside of a production plant because of its impacts on employes. Also, open house events and regular programs for handling visitors encourage tidy industrial housekeeping. Why should a modern business house itself in individual offices which look like monkish cells, or factories reminiscent of antiquated coal mines?

The public reads advertisements in publications; on posters and displays in common carriers, stores, and exhibitions; outdoor advertising and labels on packages. It sees pictures and stories in newspapers, magazines, books, and pamphlets. It watches, in increasing numbers, the pictures and hears the messages of television. What the public sees and hears repeatedly it tends to believe.

Some humans are primarily eye-minded and others ear-minded. Many people react more to word of mouth communication than to any other medium. They understand a message better when spoken than when read. Of course, a large percentage of the public represents a combination of receptiveness to oral and visual approaches.

Word-of-mouth is considered by many experts to be the most powerful carrier of ideas. This factor is reinforced tremendously by television, radio, and sound motion pictures and sound slide film.

The human body and nervous system constitute a kind of tuning fork. Some sounds please and others irritate. Noise abatement in large offices and in factories usually raises morale and productivity of workers.

Unpleasant sights, noises, and odors bother employes, communities, and visitors. Public relations leads the way in relief for such negatives.

Public relations starts *from within*. So consideration of devices to offset ill will and build good will begins with the environment of a management and its employes, its neighbors, its visitors and casual passersby. The next step consists of devices for communicating with or influencing the general or special publics beyond the inner ring.

The Promotional "Week"

Several available check lists of devices assist you to plan the dramatizing of a theme and carrying out the strategy. These lists reveal successful methods of the past. Some of the methods can be almost exactly duplicated and obtain the desired ends. But a "carbon copy" project will not frequently gain maximum attention. Some element of novelty should be injected. It is difficult indeed to discover an entirely original idea in a world with so many fertile minds. But the permutations and combinations of treatment of devices for presenting an idea may never end.

Among the commonest ways for gaining public attention is the use of a "week." It may be anything from prune week to letter-writing week or brotherhood week. There is such a large array of these weeks that frequently a harried editorial writer will ridicule the latest announcement of such an event. But an old device of this kind can be adapted effectively if given an element of freshness, if made interesting to the public, and if followed up with sufficient action and promotion.

For instance, examine the case of Oil Progress Week. The American Petroleum Institute picked up the old technique and created a yearly event with great scope and impact. It is supported by widespread advertising and publicity. In addition to a national advertising program, tie-in advertising and other promotional material is provided for oil men throughout the country.

Luncheons or dinners are given in various parts of the country. Open house events welcome the public with open arms. Attention of the general public and special publics pinpoints for several days each year upon the petroleum industry, its services to individuals and to the nation, and its sweeping progress on behalf of everyone.

Some promotional weeks have become well established and highly regarded, such as the one on fire prevention. It serves the public interest and it is well presented and supported. But some others seem rather lame excuses for promotion, not of sufficient public interest, and not adequately fortified with novelty or promotional backing.

Publicizing a New Product

Mr. Regent asked a consulting firm to help him introduce a new laundry product. He said the assignment did not involve well-rounded public relations efforts—chiefly promotional activity through publicity. His problem was how to get his brand name and national distribution established firmly ahead of expected competition.

He realized, however, the presence of public relations aspects. Every device employed should combine appeals to public interest with good taste in keeping with the reputation of his company and its older products. Each picture and news or broadcasting release should be weighed from the policy viewpoint.

When a product is really a new departure, and especially when it has novel advantages for the public, it deserves a story in publications and comment in broadcasting. So in numerous cities, as distribution spread, local news outlets informed the public about this new laundry item.

But what could be done next? The product attained national distribution rather quickly. So the announcement of this fact also roused sufficient interest to be printed and broadcast.

What then? An information service was created, which included the product's brand name, and which did research of practical help to housewives throughout the country. The material was authoritative, timely, and helpful, so publications and broadcasting stations gladly used it, giving credit to the source. The information was prepared with cooperation of research and testing laboratories and home economists.

Numerous institutes or home service centers issue releases to editors and program directors, who select the good and discard the mediocre. The device of setting up a formalized information service works well when backed by authentic and useful information and ideas, when en rapport with the media of communication to the public and the readers, viewers, or listeners, and when good judgment is used regarding timeliness and human interest values.

The information service set up for Mr. Regent next started a series of public opinion surveys in the area of homemaking related in some way to the new laundry product. One survey showed some interesting facts about the sharing between husbands and wives of chores in the average home. Many changes have occurred in these habits in the last decade or two. Therefore, an up-to-date study and report had news as well as human interest value.

Collateral Approaches

Another parade of novel devices marched out of what might be called collateral approaches. Washing clothes in a basement or laundry room doesn't bring up a pleasant image for most women, but there are happy associated ideas. Women like to think of the end results of cleanliness and good appearance of their clothing for themselves and other members of the family. They appreciate learning tips on how to save a little time and muscular effort in doing laundry chores. They like to know the effects of new laundry products on some of the many recently introduced fabrics.

So the information service made a study of how best to wash new types of textiles. This, of course, was done in cooperation with textile experts. Instead of preparing photographs of a woman working over a laundry tub or loading and unloading a washing machine, the information service took pictures of women looking attractive in the latest fashions of dresses made from the newest fabrics. The written material gave authentic advice on how to keep the dresses clean, fresh appearing, and long lasting. Wash-

ing clothes by women, like shaving for a man, is just an unpleasant chore but also a means to a satisfactory end. So the
emphasis in the promotion featured the *result* and how best to
obtain it.

· · ·

A Wide Variety of Devices

One stock device for promoting an idea, person, or product is
to crown a queen, or to select the ten most beautiful women, a
favorite pin-up girl, or someone to be marooned with. The resulting illustrations seem to have endless outlets, especially when
some element of novelty combines with the charms of the models.
Attractive pictures of children and stories about them also appeal
to nearly everyone.

A man, woman, or child singled out for an award of some kind
usually can win public attention. People like to see other persons
get credit. Thus they experience a vicarious thrill. A group of
food manufacturers, desirous of building good will, decided to
give annual merit awards to men and women believed to have
contributed the most to the advancement of nutrition. The
awards gave deserved credit to the nutrition experts and interested
many editors and readers. The good work which the manufacturers themselves did for better nutrition for the public was im-
plied by the activity.

Devices which interest opinion leaders and other thoughtful
persons include seminars, speeches, and brochures. Some advertising campaigns aim specifically at men and women who do
serious reading and who influence opinions of other persons.

Company S, in the pharmaceutical business, had scrupulously
avoided publicizing itself. Finally, it realized that its more aggressive competitors had gained ground with public opinion. So its

management decided to make up for lost time. To do so, it adopted a strategy of employing what might be called "high visibility" devices which attracted quick and favorable attention. For instance, at exhibitions and at meetings attended by its present and potential customers, it "stole the show" because of its genius in planning and operating outstanding displays.

An Investigation and Report

Merck & Co., Inc., after years of research and investment of millions of dollars, developed *Cortone,* the Merck brand of cortisone, a drug relieving human suffering from rheumatoid arthritis and many other ailments. Clinical tests had been highly encouraging and the new drug was widely acclaimed in the medical profession and by science writers.

But the necessary raw materials were scarce. The manufacturing process was long and difficult. Finally a small amount of the drug was distributed to be sold under doctors' prescriptions.

The demand greatly exceeded the limited supplies. Rumors of black markets exacting exorbitant prices for the drug appeared in the press.

The manufacturer has an unusually high reputation for integrity as well as for moderation in its pricing. It took prompt action.

It launched a thorough investigation to run down rumors of any excessive charges and diversion of the drug from proper channels.

Then it told the facts to the professions by letter and to the public generally through advertisements and publicity—why the shortage came about and how it would be remedied soon by new facilities being rushed to completion. It stated the recommended current price, which had followed repeated reductions as increased production had made them possible.

The investigation and the report practically ended the confusion which had existed. In fact, these two steps received high praise from many sources.

Other Dramatic Methods

Company T arranged seminars on subjects which tied in with the most up-to-date thought in its industry—in fact, looking well into the future. These seminars attracted outstanding speakers and discussion leaders, who in turn drew excellent audiences. The speeches were widely quoted in the press. Within a few years, Company T, which had been considered old and too conservative, was generally regarded as highly progressive—which it indeed was.

A group of American match manufacturers wanted the public to realize that persons who use book matches get most of them free. Book matches are given away almost everywhere cigarettes, cigars, and pipe tobacco are sold. The cost is covered by the book match advertising, which has strong pulling power, according to a recent national survey. But the persons who get the free matches come to take them for granted like air or like water at a public drinking fountain.

So a special device was created. Arrangements were made with a big department store which gave away thousands of book matches with the tobacco products sold to the public. Clerks were instructed to inform purchasers, "Sorry, we don't give away free matches any more."

Candid camera pictures showed the expressions on the customers' faces. Some looked as though they thought, "What next?" Others acted startled or amazed. A few argued, talked of suing, or merely turned red with anger. In each case a representative of the match people quickly explained to the purchaser that it was just a demonstration, gave him some matches, and asked permission to use the photograph in order to inform the public how much it has taken free book matches for granted.

Many other devices have been successfully employed to bridge the gap between public relations strategy and theme and their effective dramatization to the public. There are press parties, proclamations, pageants, and many other techniques.

Some methods are so extensive and expensive that the word "device" seems too weak. For instance, buildings and exhibits at world's fairs reputedly have cost millions of dollars. Special advertising campaigns, national contests with large prizes, and promotional caravans touring the nation require a "mint of money." Still they are merely devices to convey ideas to the public.

In Review

All your careful research, your isolation of problems, and your evolving of strategy and theming have little value unless you follow through and employ methods which will transmit ideas to the people who should know about them.

To do this, you should check whatever human beings observe with their eyes concerning offices, factories, products, and any other visible things, such as printed material of all kinds.

Some people are largely ear-minded or a combination of ear-minded and eye-minded. Ideas spread like wildfire through conversation or in broadcasting and sound motion pictures.

In planning devices for influencing people, you start internally and work outward. Begin with the things noticeable through the senses, especially sight and hearing, which affect a management, its workers, and its neighborhood. Then fan out to the special publics or general publics affecting your enterprise or cause.

Devices which seem designed only for attracting attention to an idea, or to the name of a company or product, involve public relations in almost every step. For enduring good will each device should be thought through for long range effects. Does it indicate integrity and good taste, as well as awareness of service and human nature? Is it newsworthy? Is the source authoritative and hence trustworthy? Does it show how to ease or shorten unpleasant chores? Does it put the spotlight on the desirable end result instead of dreary preliminary steps?

There are check lists of devices successful in the past. A few examples of such devices appear in this chapter. Some build good will through implication or through association of ideas. Some approach the general public indirectly by influencing molders of opinion who in turn spread ideas.

Other devices get quick action through their high visibility. Still others rely on negatives—showing how people would suffer if a taken-for-granted service suddenly disappeared.

The main point is that dramatic measures usually are essential in solving a problem. They should be interesting, have news value, or render practical service.

CHAPTER XIII } Rounding Out a Program

THIS BOOK highspots the steps that precede the carrying out of a program. The preliminaries search for the real problem or problems; construct a strategy, which may necessitate dissolving abuses; create a theme and devices which illustrate or dramatize it. Now we come to a final phase of the planning—fitting everything together into an orderly program.

Such a program should keep its sights aimed on solving the problem, not straying, something easy to do. The plan also should adhere closely to the strategy and theme. Of course, refinements can be made anywhere along the line, and a new, appropriate idea can be worked into the program. It is best to stick to a basic strategy but allow leeway for changes in tactics. New opportunities and problems keep popping up and you must be "quick on your feet."

A program should have some fairly simple idea to implant in the minds of the publics you try to influence. Sometimes you can fit it into a few words, as many advertisers do. The idea should be descriptive and offer a definite impression when passed along to the public. One useful method is to write a 50-word telegram telling what you want your public to know and believe.

As in advertising, good public relations depends upon repetition to impress the public. An important executive headed a campaign to put federal income taxes on a pay-as-you-go basis. He and others kept pounding away on the same idea in speeches, interviews, and statements in the press and over the radio. If only one speech had been made, scarcely a ripple would have been noticed in public opinion. But by a continuous stirring of the waters, the supporters of the movement caused the government to pay attention and to act.

Variety, Timing, and Spacing

To maintain public interest, you need to find varied approaches. For instance, advocates of the work of the Hoover Commission for governmental economy discussed a wide variety of ways to handle public funds efficiently and with minimum waste. But the approaches all tied together with the central purpose.

Devices to transmit an idea to a public should be carefully timed and spaced. July and August usually are poor months for promotion of an idea requiring heavy thinking, but Spring and Autumn offer good opportunities. Around the Christmas holiday period most people think with their hearts instead of their minds.

Even the days of the week call for study of changes in habits and minds and emotions. Many people react somewhat differently on Saturday and Sunday contrasted with Wednesday or Thursday. However, at any season of the year or day of the week or hour of the day the public pays attention to humor, pictures, human interest features, news of the entertainment world, sports, capsuled round-ups of news, or digests of the best current literature.

Ring Lardner in a visit with a group of journalism students told them not to pack laughs too closely together. "Spread them out," he said, "or your public will get tired. Also it will think of you as a 'smarty-pants' and an amateur."

So space your approaches to the public carefully. The persons who manage the means of communication realize the value of this. Mr. Stephenson, head of a large corporation, gave an average of four major speeches in a span of 12 months. Each speech was at a meeting which provided a powerful springboard for publicity.

His talks interested the audiences and, over their shoulders, some of the general public. Hence the resulting headlines in the press were deserved. Sometimes radio networks broadcast the talks or portions of them.

In an opinion survey regarding Mr. Stephenson's speeches, people were asked how many they thought he gave each year. The median reply was 20, instead of the correct answer of four.

Sound Budgeting

A vital factor in programming is the budget. One public relations firm undertook an assignment for $25,000. But $50,000 could not have satisfied what the client wanted and expected. On the other hand, another firm overestimated its client's requirements and set a figure twice as high as the budget later arrived at for a continuing program.

In public relations work sound accounting ranks high. To many people public relations still seems, more or less, a mystery. So, it should be made as understandable as possible, both in budgeting and in providing evidence of worthwhile results.

Publics and Media

Planning a program demands thoughtful defining of publics to be influenced. Literature on this subject abounds in books and magazine articles. In this book we point out just a few top level things to watch for.

Our formula for solving a public relations problem might well have included chapters devoted entirely to analysis of publics and means for reaching them. We have scattered phases of the subject through various chapters, because knowledge of publics enters into each step of the formula. However, at this point some of the highspots will be mentioned.

The general public comprises hundreds of publics with special

interests. Many of these overlap. To reach all of them would require getting in touch personally with practically everyone who
has passed beyond the infant stage. To do this would exceed the
facilities of any organization. Therefore, you select your publics
carefully.

Let's glance through a partial list of the multitudinous groupings, interests, and characteristics which collectively make up the
general public:

Male and female; age groups—children, teen-age, adults, both
young and elderly; native and foreign backgrounds; race, creed,
education, and geography—sectional, farm, town, city, or suburb;
type of job, income, politics, hobbies, and countless others.

Millions of persons live in institutions and cannot work. Usually many persons are temporarily out of a job. Migratory workers
move with the seasons and the crops, and hence are difficult to
reach consistently. Uncounted thousands have an allergy to work
of any kind and join the hobo ranks.

One organization wants to influence favorably the thinking of
essentially all adults and teen-age youths in the United States
regarding the economic system under which the nation has pros-
pered. No private organization would have access to sufficient
funds needed to tell this story individually to well over 100 million persons. How should it try, for instance, to reach Tom, who
happens to be a member of a labor union? Tom likes to read a
newspaper published by his union but, also, he scans a general
newspaper rather thoroughly. He enjoys certain shows on his
television set and others on his radio and, he likes the movies. He
devours comics but also pores over technical articles in trade
magazines and digests of serious magazine features. As a member
of the Elks, he absorbs the contents of that fraternal order's magazine, and he drops in at the club for visits with his brother Elks.

Since boyhood he has collected stamps and coins, so he keeps up-to-date on those subjects. His wife and children keep him keenly interested in homemaking and family problems to the extent that he peeks into a national women's magazine his wife subscribes for, and he reads newspaper ads announcing specials in foods, drugs, and other products. Regarding himself as a member of one political party, he still splits his ticket at the polls and therefore pays attention to facts and claims about candidates and issues. We could go much further in describing Tom and would end up by finding he isn't a type at all—he is a fairly complex individual, just as nearly everyone else is, whether on a farm, in a mine, store, office, government job, or factory, or in retirement. Each person has his own peculiar and varied interests.

So, on the surface it looks rather hopeless to reach and influence all these people. Finding *common denominators* for broad mass or large group appeals and selection of special media or methods best suited for the purposes at hand reveal the secret of some of the best solutions.

The greatest common denominator turns out to be that each member of the public is a *person*. He may raise poultry, serve as a roustabout for an oil company, or sell insurance. But being a person ranks first.

As a person he naturally relates public problems to his own interests and those of people and situations close to himself. He seldom pays much attention to an academic discussion of economics. But he listens when someone he can respect interprets economics in terms of his own job, his family, his neighbors, and his future, and factors directly impinging upon it.

In this instance, the organization desirous of educating the public on sound economic theory and practice may elect to concentrate its limited efforts into just one channel. This may take the form of preparing and promoting educational courses by each employer, on company time, tying economics to the individual enterprise and each person associated with it. Such efforts have mushroomed in the United States in recent years and they seem effectual. They have influenced many "Toms."

Public relations does not rely entirely upon editorial material in publications and broadcasting, or motion pictures and advertising, important as all these media have become. A vast amount of educational work, however, does rely upon these more obvious means of communications. The organization used in this example might train all of its guns at publications or at broadcasting or both. Or it might try an indirect approach through the media of lectures, seminars, or specialized magazine articles influencing opinion molders.

•   •   •

One dog food manufacturer wanted to get a message implanted in the minds of all owners of dogs. He discovered that in the United States the total number of dogs probably equals or surpasses the number of adult males. He lacked the funds to conduct an educational campaign upon such a vast scale. So he compromised by telling his story to all veterinarians by direct mail literature and by publicity and advertising in trade and professional publications.

A small pharmaceutical company considered the idea of publicizing its name to the general public but lacked sufficient promotional funds for such an ambitious project. So the company promoted its ideas among physicians, pharmacists, educators, and others who directly or indirectly influence much of the public.

One industrial association set its sights too low. Its limited public relations program primarily talked to its own membership. Then it woke up to the fact that it should tell its story to the public at large on a grand scale in order to solve a major problem.

A foundation, with a small fund for an educational program,

chose as its target certain writers of syndicated columns appearing in many newspapers. The foundation, as a result of its research, turned over findings from time to time to the columnists who liked and commented favorably upon the material.

Some of the largest corporations and associations tie in with almost every type of medium reaching the public. This includes paid advertising in publications and in broadcasting; direct mail literature; materials for teachers' use in classrooms and program directors of clubs; speakers' bureaus; motion pictures, posters, and other channels.

Make sure to comprehend the needs of editors and other directors of media. Miss Thomson, a beginner in publicity work, wrote an article for a trade paper. The editor returned it with the comment that it merely puffed up a certain company. The article would be acceptable if rewritten to serve the readers by inspiring, informing, or even entertaining them or by providing them with ideas they might adopt or adapt. Miss Thomson thus learned one of the primary principles of journalism and public relations.

Word-of-mouth communication is powerful but hard to organize. A classic example is the promotion of Ford jokes in the early days of the motorcar industry. In the business world most of the "whispering campaigns" probably have sprung up more or less by accident. In the political field, there no doubt has been organized sponsorship, but this is difficult to trace. In any event, try to find constructive ways of tapping the power of word-of-mouth communication.

• • •

Now let's examine the chief media for reaching the general public and special publics.

Newspapers: An estimated 93 per cent of our adult population reads newspapers—providing quick, flexible coverage of events and other subjects of interest to the readers. In this field, the competent publicist can serve as an extra assistant to editors. Moreover, various other media often pick up story ideas from items in the newspapers.

One factor to consider in building a list for a publicity project is the frequency and the time of issue. That is, one should determine whether papers are dailies (morning or afternoon), semi-weeklies, weeklies, or weekend publications. If you give a story to the morning papers, for example, often it should be rewritten for evening paper release. The weekend publications, and their supplements frequently allow more lengthy treatment of an important story.

Another factor is the coverage of a paper—whether it is metropolitan or it serves one or several adjoining counties. The hometown paper is likely to have a different editorial outlook from the big city daily, and the neighborhood weekly will differ from both.

The type of readership should be considered. It may be a general paper or specialize in business or financial news. It may be conservative, left-wing, labor, or liberal. There also are the foreign language press, the Negro press, the college press, and other special interest press, such as *Variety* or *Women's Wear Daily*.

Still another item of importance to the public relations worker is the department of the newspaper that would be most concerned with his material. Such departments include the woman's page, or the financial, business, sports, amusement, science, society, or editorial page or column. And not to be forgotten is the "letters to the editor" column which can be useful to the publicist.

One factor influencing the method of handling any given story is the type of material. It may be a spot news item, it may merit "feature" treatment, or it may be a filler—something the editor would use at the end of a column to make it the proper length.

Wire Services: Fast and economical, the wire services should be used on news of state-wide, sectional, or national interest or importance. Three of the major wire services are Associated Press, United Press, and International News Service.

All the important dailies, plus radio and TV stations, pick up news from at least one of these wire services. And a great many small city papers get their news from these sources.

Wire services gather news chiefly from correspondents in principal cities here and abroad. But suitable news items are welcomed direct from the publicist.

Picture and Feature Syndicates: Picture syndicates are always looking for good, newsworthy photos, some of which they send by wire or by mail to member newspapers and magazines. Be sure, however, that you offer the syndicates only outstanding pictures of widespread interest. Technically, your photos should be suitable for transmission by wire, and they should be flexible enough for easy make-up by the editor—he may be able to allow you only one column, rather than the two-column spread you hoped for.

The major photo syndicates include the Associated Press and its subsidiary, World Wide Photos; International News Pictures, and Acme Newspictures. They maintain offices in the larger cities.

There are hundreds of feature and private syndicates which handle a wide variety of material: jokes, cartoons, comic strips, and beauty aids; science and financial news; serialized novels and how-to-make or how-to-do-it pieces. Some syndicates will sell you mat services, from which weeklies and small dailies obtain—"for free"—features, news items, and artwork they usually can't afford to buy.

Broadcasting—Radio and TV: Radio is essentially a personality medium, blessed with the magic of sound effects and, in the case of TV, both sound and sight. At any single time broadcasting networks reach a huge audience almost instantaneously—for example, the broadcast of signing the Japanese peace treaty at San Francisco, or a Rose Bowl game.

On sustaining time, which is not paid for by a sponsor, when your material is of sufficient interest or value, you can often take part or get mention on the programs. Occasionally, there are opportunities for arranging interviews on farm, women's service, and other similar programs and forums. And occasionally you can demonstrate a new product on service-type TV shows. And then there's always the possibility, with especially newsworthy material, that you may stage a special event for broadcast coverage.

Magazines: At first, a person is likely to be baffled by the size and complexity of the magazine field. According to a U. S. Department of Commerce study, approximately 5,000 periodicals are published in the U. S. Their circulations range from a high of more than 10 million to a low of a few hundred. The overall total is in the neighborhood of 400 million—which obviously involves multiple readership. The range of interests covered by periodicals is vast. Within any interest grouping, no two magazines are edited alike. In working with magazines, the public relations practitioner has the time element in his favor, for many periodicals largely are developed two or three issues ahead of publication date.

For your "big break" in the magazine field—the feature story —it is best to "rifle shot" your material. But with items of relatively broad interests, such as startling new product announcements, you may be quite successful using a well-aimed shotgun.

In planning feature material, you should consider first the type of magazine at which you are aiming and the interests for which it is edited. Following are four categories you want to study:

1. *General, national periodicals*—These include news and picture weeklies and monthlies, and general interest magazines. Widespread coverage of your stories in the daily press is often helpful to success with these periodicals.
2. *Special interest publications*—These include: fiction, women's, home and gardening, foreign language, labor, fashion, teen-age and juvenile, farming, hobbies, religious, and fraternal. Also included are the education press—college and high school publications.
3. *Business, financial, and professional periodicals*—With these, the editors are looking for ideas and information for their readers to adapt profitably to their business or profession.
4. *Company publications*—Central Feature News Service, which publishes *Feature,* estimates conservatively that 9,000 "house organs" are published in the United States. At least 20 have circulations over 1 million and the overall is between 60 and 75 million. Material directed to internal house organs should be angled to interest or help the employe, while material for external ones should promote in some way the prestige, products, or services of the company publishing them, as well as serving the average reader.

When you want to approach a certain magazine about a story, study carefully its format and the particular audience for which it is edited. Find out, if you can, whether it is mainly staff-written, or whether it uses ideas or material from free-lance writers and public relations practitioners.

Mention should be made of the value of free-lance writers. They know their markets and their editors well. By seeing your material from an editor's viewpoint, they can be helpful in your efforts to serve in the magazine field.

Additional Printed Media: Foregoing are several of the chief media available to the public relations man. There are numerous others, and they all have their own special value in a well-rounded program. Here are some examples: Newsletters, comics, pamphlets, posters, bulletins, dodgers, door-knob tags, lapel buttons, auto bumper strips, theater and railroad tickets, timetables, envelope stuffers, catalogs, books, clipsheets. The possibilities are limited chiefly to your needs, your budget, and your ingenuity.

The Spoken Word: Forms of oral communications include lectures, speeches, demonstrations, telephone campaigns.

Other Media: This includes the whole gamut of audio-visual media—motion picture films and slide films (both sound and silent), exhibits, contests, conventions and trade fairs, and numerous others you may develop as the need arises.

•   •   •

We have tried to indicate briefly some of the factors influencing your choice of media, whether for public relations advertising or for publicity.

Your success in public relations communication is related directly to the manner in which you *serve* those who control and administer media. You must view your material objectively through *their* eyes. Offer them only that which will help them and their audiences, as they see it; don't bother them with material they cannot or should not use, and don't expect them to do your work.

There are many sources from which you can build media lists. Among the more important are:

1. *Editor and Publisher International Yearbook,* published in New York City. It covers daily and Sunday newspapers, syndicates, departmental editors, etc.

2. *Annual Directory of Syndicated Features,* published by Editor & Publisher, New York City.

3. *Directory of Newspapers and Periodicals,* by N. W. Ayer & Sons, Philadelphia.

4. *Annual Directory of County and Suburban Hometown Newspapers,* by the American Press Association, New York City. It covers weeklies, semi-weeklies, etc.

5. *Standard Rate and Data,* Inc., Evanston, Ill., has a Consumer Magazine section, which also covers farm publications, and a business publications section. Though these are primarily listings of space rates, they can be very useful in building publicity lists. *Standard Rate and Data* also has sections on radio, television, weekly newspapers, daily newspapers, and transportation media.

6. *Printer's Ink Directory of House Organs,* New York City.

7. *Blue Book of Magazine Writers,* covers leading freelance writers. It is published by Central Feature News, Inc., New York City.

8. *Broadcasting* year book, published in Washington, D. C., covers radio and television.

9. *Radio and TV Personalities Directory,* by Radio Reports, Inc., New York City.

10. *Patterson's American Educational Directory,* published in Chicago, and directories published by the National Education Association, of Washington, D. C., cover the scholastic field.

In addition to the foregoing, you can build lists from numerous other sources. For instance, you might use the *Writer's Yearbook* and any appropriate membership list you might obtain.

And you might buy lists. By and large, selections for your media lists call for time, care, and ingenuity.

Specialists in Phases of Public Relations

Naturally, your programming must rely on the men and women available to do the work. One consulting firm, excellent in communicating ideas to the general public, when asked to write an annual report to stockholders and a handbook for employes, lacked personnel sufficiently trained for work in stockholder and employe relations and wisely refused to undertake assignments of these kinds.

Another firm did not have personnel experienced in top-flight publicity projects aimed at the general public. This firm had skills in other fields, such as community, employe, stockholder, trade, and governmental relations. It would make a mistake if it went beyond its limitations and attempted an extensive publicity program.

With the vast expansion of the public relations field in recent years, more and more specialization takes place, just as it has in the medical profession over a much longer period. Some of the pioneer practitioners in public relations advised on all phases of human relationships, but today their firms have their own specialists or can call on them elsewhere.

For planning and operating a program you need a composite of personnel not only with special skills but also with judgment, objectivity, alertness, imagination, integrity, and a sensitivity to human interests. These qualities do not come from reading books, although books and articles should help.

Ability to Change

Watch for change of pace in a program. The basic strategy, theme, and general direction can and usually should remain constant. Most projects must be planned far in advance. But there always is need for rapid thinking and for flexibility, as conditions suddenly change and opportunities arise. A program should not be "cut and dried."

One successful magazine editor returned from a long trip. During his absence his assistants had planned some forthcoming issues utilizing ideas effective in earlier years. The war in Korea had broken out and there were sudden changes in public attitudes and interests. The editor sensed these and the magazine's plans for the next issues were altered accordingly.

Other Factors

A program should have public relations policy embedded in all steps, even some which seem like small or mechanical details. For instance, consider a short news release about a new wing of a factory, prepared for newspapers in a plant community and neighboring towns. The story may be technically correct but it may sound too cold and formal. It might well contain items of human interest and somehow show that the manufacturer likes the community in which he operates.

Whether true or not, there is a story of the Chinese doctor in olden days being paid to help *prevent* a person from getting sick, instead of merely helping him get well. Something similar may apply to public relations counseling. It should try to keep the client out of trouble and to fortify him with healthy, profitable human relationships for establishing good will.

The counselor also often serves as a fireman when the house catches fire. But public relations should not be turned on and off like a faucet. It should be inherent and never-ending. Even in such a short-range public relations project, thought should be given to impacts in the distant future as well as the present. Each step should fit into a continued story.

So, in planning a program, in its entirety and its minute parts, think of the future. One capable practitioner, in nearly every important recommendation, takes the time to think how it might look five or more years hence. Will it seem silly or will it reflect timeless good judgment and integrity?

In this short book we have stressed the *thinking* stages of public relations. In our illustrations we have demonstrated thoughts converted into action. But the analysis and planning are of utmost importance. A football team, with members physically able and mentally keen, can become a champion only with wise, thorough training, knowledge of competition, and sound strategy and tactics.

In Review

In planning a program, note such guideposts as these: Don't stray from the single-minded purpose of solving a clearcut problem or problems. Stick to a basic strategy and theme which hold up, but allow for open-mindedness and flexibility in day-to-day tactics.

In outlining what you will try to do with your public, make the goal so clearcut and simple that you can put it into a 50-word telegram.

Repeat your messages—over and over. Not many people hear you the first time. At least they don't choose to *do* anything about your ideas until it dawns upon them in a series of appealing, convincing forms.

Time and space the methods to convey thoughts to the public. The habits and interests of multitudes of people vary in fairly regular patterns depending on the hours of the day, the days of a week, and the seasons of a year. In timing and spacing, avoid excesses. People don't especially want to read or hear what you have to say, at least not at the outset. So don't expect too much of their attention, time, and effort.

A good public relations program must lean not only on sound thinking but also on finances. Success depends on a sensible combination of both elements.

Explore your publics carefully. Limitations of budgets and personnel restrict you to working only with publics which will accomplish the most for approaching your aims. On the other hand, some organizations fall far short of setting up adequate wherewithal for operations to solve their problems.

The media for reaching your publics call for comparable understanding. The directors of media of communications to the public heed you primarily for what you can contribute to serve, amuse, inspire, or otherwise appeal to their readers or listeners. Word of mouth communication, perhaps the most powerful and surely worth encouraging, is difficult to direct in an organized way.

A program should inventory the men and women available to carry it out. In the early days of modern public relations, counselors advised on almost all kinds of human relationships. Now the day of specialists has arrived. One counseling firm may have several kinds of specialists or it can find them elsewhere.

Essential qualities, such as objectivity, judgment, and character, may be affected only slightly through reading. These assets must be acquired in some way or other by a public relations worker who succeeds.

In adopting a basic formula for solving problems of human relations, you should keep everlastingly on your toes for changes going on all around us. Some of these strike almost overnight. So you should not get chained to cut-and-dried concepts and methods.

A program rests upon major and minor items, but even the

smallest may require public relations policy treatment. Try to visualize how the things you say and write might sound or look several years in the future.

The thinking which penetrates a program for solving a public relations problem is at least half the battle. So this book has concentrated on proper analysis and planning, with the realization that competent persons can carry out the program and turn in a champion performance if they have the right skills and guidance.

CHAPTER XIV } Concluding Thoughts

IN PROJECTING this book, the aim is not at the myriad technical details of public relations work but on the bull's-eye—understanding and solving problems. We concentrate on the thinking and planning up to the point where others can "run with the ball" in carrying out a program.

Dozens of examples have illustrated specific points. In squeezing them into a few sentences or paragraphs, we have had to omit important sidelights. Most of the incidents reflect accurately certain situations that the author has observed. But some are adapted to show what is typical of situations which can or do arise and what in his opinion should be done about them. All names of persons and organizations are fictitious, except where clearly identified. No attempt is made to paint a comprehensive portrait of persons or management groups, and names and symbols are used only to add a little readability.

We hope our thoughts will interest and help present and potential workers in the public relations and allied fields, and group leaders who want to learn more about analysis and solution of human relations problems.

The author's viewpoint is largely from that of business and industry and their trade associations, plus the many ramifications involved. In this connection, here is an excerpt from a statement by Arthur W. Page, business consultant and former vice president in charge of public relations of the American Telephone and Telegraph Company, in *Introduction to Public Relations,* by Dave Hyatt, Extension Bulletin ⅍5, New York

State School of Industrial and Labor Relations, Cornell University, September, 1950:

> "All business in a democratic country begins with public permission and exists by public approval. If that is true, it follows that business should be cheerfully willing to tell the public what its policies are, what it is doing, and what it hopes to do."

Business and industry with far-flung public relations problems contribute to charities, schools, churches, hospitals, and countless other organizations. They have relationships with governmental agencies at every level, including the international as well as the municipal authority. They deal with masses of consumer-citizens and need to understand basic factors concerning the thoughts and emotions of these people.

Early in this book some definitions of public relations are given. Still another definition plus some interesting remarks are contained in the following quotation from an editorial in *Tide*, December 14, 1951:

> "Today more businessmen, ordinary and otherwise, have 'bought' the public relations concept and put it into practice. And more of them understand public relations, at least in its simplest form —'doing good and getting credit for it.'

> "What many still do not understand, however, is that good public relations means, needs and requires positive thinking. That means that you must stand for something, that you must expand your horizon beyond merely the opposition to other things or other people's ideas. Unless you are willing to take a positive kind of position, you are not practicing good public relations; you are just going through some motions that don't mean very much."

Before applying a formula for solving a public relations problem, there are some essential preliminaries. One of the first of these is to grasp the nature of public relations or to get the aid of someone who can provide guidance. Some group leaders think the power of public relations should be applied only in the form of a coat of attractive paint to cover up something unsightly, without regard to correction of defects in the structure behind the paint.

Too many persons or organizations use public relations techniques to "mop up" after mistakes have dirtied the floor, rather than to take advantage of the much more valuable aspect, which is to *anticipate* probable public reactions to some statement or action.

One must have some understanding of himself as a human being with his ambitions, fears, and other powerful emotions, if he is to acquire *objectivity* in his own judgments and in understanding other people, both as individuals and groups. He should have a realization of the great struggle going on within people adjusting themselves—or failing to do so—to modern conditions changing so rapidly that it is difficult for human nature to catch up. This applies to our jobs and to our feelings of insecurity regarding threats of inflation, atomic warfare, and frightening doctrines.

Modern trends include the switch from rural to urban living; the changing nature of social, economic, and professional groupings, and vast alterations of many kinds which have occurred in the space of a single decade. The shift of scenery has been so marked that few are aware of its total nature.

For instance, there are the higher rate, and younger average age of marriage; the amazing increase in home ownership and everything involved with it; a strengthening of family life among most young people, with larger families and more home attractions—deterred somewhat by the fact that so many married women now have part- or full-time paid jobs.

An upheaval in routines in the homes has accompanied the

influx of modern labor saving devices and rearrangement of household duties, at a time when domestic servants have become scarce. The nation's assets are being turned over to women rapidly. At the same time more infants are arriving, people live much longer. Television helps to create a revoluton in habits and in impacts on the human mind. Gratification for the advances of modern transportation, communication, science, and other fields is dampened by the increased pall of fear and foreboding. But there are probably as many optimistic as pessimistic signs all around us—more sanity and balance, including tolerance, especially among young people, and recognition of the merits and opportunities of the bases of American life—its social and economic system and its international responsibilities. There are indications of a possible awakening to moral, spiritual, and religious values, and revulsion against complacency and corruption in high places.

Another preliminary step for anyone who wishes to utilize public relations knowledge is to observe the fund of wisdom and experience in the field of journalism, which generally is regarded as an excellent training ground as well as being a powerful force in its own right. The many values of journalistic training, eighteen mentioned earlier in this book, are too numerous to detail in this summary. But they should be recognized by anyone who wishes to have a good background for public relations.

A Formula for Solving a Public Relations Problem

After acquiring much of the desirable background outlined in the preceding pages, you can apply a formula for finding out the true nature of a public relations problem and developing a program for solving it. Frequently you will need an experienced practitioner to assist you.

You may have seen a demonstration by a mathematical wizard.

Through special ability and practice he can add or subtract, multiply or divide almost astronomical figures in the twinkling of an eye. No matter how rapidly he does the trick, certain mental processes must be applied, even though they seem to be raced through with the speed of light.

On some occasions, a public relations counselor has given, on the spur of the moment, a fortunate suggestion for the solution of a problem without apparent use of any formalized process of analysis or synthesis. Actually, he telescoped previous experiences, judgments, and "know-how" rapidly.

To apply a sound formula usually calls for thorough fact-finding and development of procedures. After getting a basic understanding of public relations functions and other valuable background knowledge, here are steps in a formula (with allowances, of course, for exceptional conditions) which has been highly successful:

1. Interviewing

Interview, individually and in groups, persons who can give you facts or opinions which will help to clarify problems and give clues to solutions.

a. *The "What, Who, When, Where, Why" Method*
To conduct these interviews you need certain simple check lists which you can carry in your head in order to cover all principal aspects. The first of these consists of the five W's of journalism—what, who, when, where, and why.

b. *"Mind, Spirit, Body, and Society" Questions*
Another check list is "mind, spirit, body, and society." These points cover broad areas. For instance, "body" refers not only to physical factors concerning individuals, but also material things such as products, plants, equipment, and supplies.

c. *Check list of Major Functions and Activities*

Still another formula for interviewing and other research deals with the major functions and activities of an organization, including the basic product, service, or idea; the management; financing; sales and advertising; manufacturing; research; human relations, and several others. You may build a more elaborate check list covering less obvious subjects which may turn out to be of value.

2. Reading

In addition to interviews, a great deal of reading may be required—before, between, and following the interviews. In doing such reading, you can use the same check lists suggested for interviews, plus other subjects which may have a bearing on the problem and its solution. Be selective in your reading, because much of it can be wasted. Concentrate on essentials, especially by skim reading hundreds of pages, many of which may be quite sterile from your viewpoint. Improve your memory for key facts or thoughts and learn how to find correct answers to many kinds of questions quickly. Learn how to boil down masses of material to essentials and how to "read between the lines" in cautiously written reports.

3. Using Opinion Research

Frequently formal opinion research discloses the true nature of a problem or problems in human relations. Such research usually gives clues of incalculable value in the follow-up strategy and program. No head of an organization can really know the attitudes and feelings of a large number of other individuals without intelligent diagnosis. This applies to employes, communities, distributors and dealers, stockholders, customers, suppliers, governmental contacts, and the general public. In this book we have offered ten specific suggestions regarding opinion research as it applies to public relations. An added general thought is that you should use opinion research as part of a sturdy foundation for a public relations project, but not as a substitute for perception and judgment.

4. Clearing Out Non-Essentials

Many problems are almost completely blacked-out by non-essentials which seem crucial to those closest to them. To get to the heart of a problem use the process of elimination. Clear away the underbrush of concern only to insiders before considering ideas to present to special publics or the general public. Get rid of concepts of doubtful truth or assumptions not sustained by adequate reasoning or facts. Rule out ideas built up from roused emotions or concentration on subjectivity. Techniques successful in the past need adapting in order to succeed in the light of changed conditions. Live in the present and future instead of the past. Don't hesitate to cut a Gordian knot in a complicated situation and stick to one simple solution which makes sense. Try to co-ordinate conflicting viewpoints in a fair and reasonable manner.

5. Shaping Strategy

In developing strategy, first determine abuses or misunderstandings needing correction. Divert attention from bad to good symbols. Talk in the language and interests of your publics and do it in a calm, reasoning, friendly manner. An advocate aroused emotionally or one who seems unduly to further his personal interests is likely to be discounted or ignored. The public welcomes actions or statements by persons or organizations obviously working not only for their own reasonable interests but also for those of the public's.

In creating a major shift in public opinion, there often needs to be an intermediate phase during which people become open-minded and willing to consider both sides of a controversy. Don't spend your effort in ridicule of an adversary, but concentrate on selling your own viewpoint. Understand your publics' attitudes thoroughly but recognize that they sometimes err and can be redirected. Still, if you get too far ahead, the parade you lead may go straight forward when you turn a corner. Rely on widely-accepted symbols, such as good sportsmanship and teamwork, if they apply to the cause you promote.

6. Finding a Theme

A theme symbolizes your messages simply and effectively to the public or publics to be influenced, whereas a strategy may be too complicated for quick comprehension except to a management. Every enterprise which has won acceptance from the public over a considerable period must have within itself some element symbolical of its objectives or valuable products or services. A theme should express a truth and keep in step with the public's interests. Reiterate it constantly and support it by performance.

7. Dramatizing with Devices

Devices dramatize a strategy and theme. Without dramatization to the public, all your preparatory work of analysis of a problem and strategy and theming may prove fruitless. These devices appeal to human senses, primarily seeing and hearing. A device should not be an isolated phenomenon but part of an integrated program designed for a certain effect, usually for building both short and long range good will. To achieve this worthy end a dramatic technique should attract attention but it should not involve bad taste. It should contain news value or other human interest. Or it may amuse, instruct, or render service. Many methods of previous years may be repeated successfully, especially with some novel treatment or timeliness.

8. Rounding Out a Program

In rounding out a program, after analysis of the problem and formation of strategy, theme, and devices, consider several factors—novelty, timing, and spacing; personnel and budgetary needs and limitations; ability to make a desirable change of pace.

Unusual attention must be given to defining and understanding your publics and the best media for reaching them. There are wide variations in the interests of an individual. And there are far too many media for any one organization to use all of them. So a great deal of study and judgment is needed in *selection* of the publics and the channels for approaching and influencing them. The selecting of publics and media could have been made a step in our formula (or even the basis for an entire volume). But instead, this subject was distributed through various chapters of this book.

Adhere to your definite objectives at all times, even though some of the methods seem collateral approaches to your goals. Good public relations policy should penetrate every detail of a program.

Always keep alert to new ideas, to changes, to opportunities. Try to foresee how the things you do or say will look or sound several years hence. Good public relations is not here today and gone next week. It should be a continuous and farsighted activity for the benefit of those who apply its power and above all for those on the receiving end—men, women, and children everywhere.

·   ·   ·

So, as a final round-up of a formula for solving public relations problems, we have condensed the major steps into the following space small enough to keep in a pocket and sufficiently brief to carry in a person's head:

A Formula for Solving a Public Relations Problem

(To apply this one first should have (a) an understanding of the basic nature of public relations and (b) sufficient background knowledge of human nature and conditions which affect human attitudes.)

1. Interviewing
   a. The "What, Who, When, Where, Why" Method
   b. "Mind, Spirit, Body, and Society" Questions
   c. Check list of Major Functions and Activities
2. Reading
3. Opinion Research
4. Clearing Out Non-Essentials
5. Shaping Strategy
6. Finding a Theme
7. Dramatizing with Devices
8. Rounding Out a Program

---

3 5282 00092 9615